100 YEARS
OF EICHENDORFF SONGS

RECENT RESEARCHES IN THE MUSIC OF THE NINETEENTH
AND EARLY TWENTIETH CENTURIES

Rufus Hallmark, general editor

A-R Editions, Inc., publishes six quarterly series—

Recent Researches in the Music of the Middle Ages and Early Renaissance,
Margaret Bent, general editor;

Recent Researches in the Music of the Renaissance,
James Haar and Howard Mayer Brown, general editors;

Recent Researches in the Music of the Baroque Era,
Robert L. Marshall, general editor;

Recent Researches in the Music of the Classical Era,
Eugene K. Wolf, general editor;

Recent Researches in the Music of the Nineteenth and Early Twentieth Centuries,
Rufus Hallmark, general editor;

Recent Researches in American Music,
H. Wiley Hitchcock, general editor—

which make public music that is being brought to light
in the course of current musicological research.

Each volume in the *Recent Researches* is devoted
to works by a single composer or to a single genre of composition,
chosen because of its potential interest to scholars and performers,
and prepared for publication according to the standards that govern
the making of all reliable historical editions.

Subscribers to this series, as well as patrons of subscribing institutions,
are invited to apply for information about the "Copyright-Sharing Policy"
of A-R Editions, Inc., under which the contents of this volume
may be reproduced free of charge for study or performance.

Correspondence should be addressed:

A-R EDITIONS, INC.
315 West Gorham Street
Madison, Wisconsin 53703

RECENT RESEARCHES IN THE MUSIC OF THE NINETEENTH
AND EARLY TWENTIETH CENTURIES • VOLUME V

100 YEARS OF EICHENDORFF SONGS

Edited by Jurgen Thym

A-R EDITIONS, INC. • MADISON

To

Jan deGaetani

and

Thomas Paul

Distinguished Performers and Colleagues

at the

Eastman School of Music

© 1983 by A-R Editions, Inc.
All rights reserved
Printed in the United States of America

Library of Congress Cataloging in Publication Data:

100 years of Eichendorff songs.

   (Recent researches in the music of the nineteenth and early twentieth centuries, ISSN 0193-5364 ; v.5)
   Songs on poems by Joseph Eichendorff ; German words.
   Prefatory notes include texts with English translations.
   Includes bibliographical notes.
   Contents: Untreue / Friedrich Glück—Der Einsiedler / Joseph Dessauer—Frühlingsnacht / Friedrich Curschmann—[etc.]
   1. Songs with piano. 2. Eichendorff, Joseph, Freiherr von, 1788–1857—Musical settings. I. Eichendorff, Joseph, Freiherr von, 1788–1857. II. Thym, Jurgen. III. Title: One hundred years of Eichendorff songs. IV. Series: Recent researches in the music of the nineteenth and early twentieth centuries ; v. 5.

M2.R23834   vol. 5   [M1619.5]   83-11863
ISBN 0-89579-173-0

Contents

Preface	vii
Scope of the Edition	vii
Eichendorff's Poetry and the Nineteenth-Century *Lied*	vii
Composers and Sources	xii
Critical Commentary	xvi
Acknowledgments	xxiv
Notes	xxv
Plate I	xxviii
Plate II	xxix

[1]	Untreue	Friedrich Glück (1793–1840)	1
[2]	Der Einsiedler	Joseph Dessauer (1798–1876)	2
[3]	Frühlingsnacht (Op. 20, No. 4)	Friedrich Curschmann (1805–1841)	9
[4]	Nachtwanderer (Op. 7, No. 1)	Fanny Hensel (1805–1847)	13
[5]	Abends (Op. 16, No. 4)	Robert Franz (1815–1892)	16
[6]	Am Strom (Op. 30, No. 3)	Robert Franz	18
[7]	Der Einsiedler	Karl Reinthaler (1822–1896)	22
[8]	Ich wandre durch die stille Nacht (Op. 95)	Theodor Kirchner (1823–1903)	28
[9]	Die Kleine (Op. 37, No. 1)	Franz von Holstein (1826–1878)	30
[10]	Der Morgen (Op. 81, No. 3)	Eduard Lassen (1830–1904)	32
[11]	Waldesgespräch (Op. 5, No. 4)	Adolf Jensen (1837–1879)	35
[12]	Die Nachtblume (Op. 22, No. 2)	Joseph Rheinberger (1839–1901)	40
[13]	Lockung (Op. 22, No. 1)	Bernhard Hopffer (1840–1877)	44
[14]	Frische Fahrt (Op. 16, No. 2)	Ernst Rudorff (1840–1916)	48
[15]	Waldeinsamkeit	Philipp Spitta (1841–1894)	51
[16]	Abschied (Op. 9, No. 5)	Hans Pfitzner (1869–1949)	54
[17]	In Danzig (Op. 22, No. 1)	Hans Pfitzner	57
[18]	Nachtlied (Op. 20, No. 13)	Othmar Schoeck (1886–1957)	61
[19]	Ergebung (Op. 30, No. 6)	Othmar Schoeck	66
[20]	Marienlied	Reinhard Schwarz-Schilling (1904–)	68

Preface

Scope of the Edition

The purpose of this edition is to present a group of songs illustrating the development of the *Lied* from the middle of the nineteenth to the early twentieth century. In view of the sheer quantity and the complex dissemination of the repertoire, however, the evolution of the German *Lied* can hardly be surveyed comprehensively in a collection such as this. Thus, the editor's problem, in endeavoring to illustrate the history of the *Lied*, is to find a rationale for selecting songs from a vast and multi-faceted body of music.

Most editions of nineteenth-century songs have concentrated on one composer or on a few of the greatest. The repertoire of Schubert, Mendelssohn, Schumann, Brahms, and Wolf is known through the Peters editions of their works; representative anthologies of selected songs by Franz, Grieg, Jensen, Liszt, R. Strauß, Tchaikovsky, and some of the previously mentioned masters were published in the early twentieth century by the Oliver Ditson Company of Boston as part of *The Musician's Library*. Of this series only the Liszt volume and *Fifty Mastersongs* have been reprinted—by Dover. Many other anthologies similarly limit the repertoire by choosing songs exclusively from the output of the well-known songwriters. This concentration on the great masters leads to a rather limited view of the history of the *Lied*, since lesser-known composers also played an important role in its evolution. In fact, such composers often excelled in small, intimate musical genres such as the song.

Publishers' reluctance to make the repertoire of minor song composers available in modern editions is easily understandable. The reason is not so much fear of presenting mediocrity; the problem consists rather in finding a common denominator to unify such an anthology. Collections such as "Singer X's Favorite Songs," which do indeed exist, contain settings only loosely strung together. When lesser composers are to be included, a stronger rationale for selection becomes imperative.

A few anthologies do include single songs by little-known composers. Moser's *German Solo Song and the Ballad* (Cologne: Arno Volk-Verlag, 1958) and Stephenson's *Romanticism in Music* (Cologne: Arno Volk-Verlag, 1961), both in the Anthology of Music series, are two such examples. By selecting songs to illustrate points in commentaries dealing with the evolution of a genre or concept, the editors manage to present a few lesser-known songwriters with one composition each. Another avenue has been chosen by Friedlaender (*Gedichte von Goethe in Kompositionen*, 2 vols., Weimar: Verlag der Goethe-Gesellschaft, 1896 and 1916) and Komma (*Lieder und Gesänge nach Dichtungen von Friedrich Hölderlin*, Tübingen: J. C. B. Mohr, 1967); both editors have chosen settings of texts by a single poet, written by various composers over a period of time, as a common denominator of their anthologies.

Such an approach would seem to be more beneficial to performers and scholars than compiling a collection of settings that lacks a unifying feature altogether. Singers have found it advantageous to plan recitals in which at least a group of songs, if not the whole program, is unified by a common idea. (Fischer-Dieskau's recording *Frühe Goethe-Lieder*, Archive 2533149, for instance, depends exclusively on selections from Friedlaender's volumes of Goethe songs.) In addition, the understanding of the evolution of the *Lied* and of principles of text-setting in the nineteenth century may be enhanced by the provision of material that allows comparative studies of musical settings of the same poem, or at least of the same type of poetry.

The present anthology, following the same principles as Friedlaender's and Komma's editions, is made up of settings of poems by Joseph Freiherr von Eichendorff. Since songs by the great masters, especially by Schumann and Wolf, are readily available, this anthology has been compiled from the works of composers not represented in standard song editions. The decision to restrict this anthology to approximately one hundred years grew quite naturally from the songs themselves; settings of Eichendorff's poems began to blossom soon after the publication of the collected poems in 1837 and found their last significant representatives in the works of descendants of late Romanticism in the first half of the twentieth century. In order to illustrate the stylistic development of the German *Lied* generally, and of Eichendorff settings in particular, the songs have been arranged in this edition in approximate chronological order according to the birth dates of the composers.

Eichendorff's Poetry and the Nineteenth-Century *Lied*

Introduction

Joseph Freiherr von Eichendorff was born into an aristocratic family on March 10, 1788, at Lubowitz castle near Ratibor (today Racibórz) in Upper Silesia. After a happy and carefree childhood on his family's estate, he studied law at the Universities of Halle and Heidelberg, where he was exposed to the ideas of German literary Romanticism, most notably through Professors Görres and Loeben. Travels through Germany, Austria, and France rounded off Eichendorff's education. The years 1813/14 saw him on the side of the liberation armies defeating Napoleon. Because of his father's bankruptcy, Eichendorff was forced to seek employment in the Prussian civil service. For the next thirty years he held administrative jobs in various provincial capitals: Breslau (today Wroclaw), Danzig (Gdańsk), Königsberg (Kaliningrad), and, finally, Berlin. Because of ill health and disagreements with the Prussian bureaucracy, he left the civil service in 1844. During his retirement, he lived at various locations, including Vienna, Dresden, and Berlin. He died on November 26, 1857, in Neisse (Silesia).

Eichendorff is one of the major figures of German literary Romanticism. His work, written mainly during vacations and in spare hours after his duties as an administrator, encompasses novels (*Ahnung und Gegenwart*, 1813; *Dichter und ihre Gesellen*, 1834), novellas (*Das Marmorbild*, 1819; *Aus dem Leben eines Taugenichts*, 1826), plays, literary and historical essays, poems, and translations of Calderon's works. It was mainly the novella *Taugenichts* and the poems that made Eichendorff widely known during his lifetime.[1]

Eichendorff is not only an important representative of German literary history but also a major figure of musical Romanticism in the nineteenth century and its descendants in the twentieth century. Ever since their first publication, Eichendorff's poems have challenged composers to set them as solo songs with piano accompaniment, as part-songs, as cantatas, as well as in other genres. Hundreds of composers were attracted by Eichendorff's lyrics and set them to music. Mendelssohn's *O Täler weit, o Höhen*, and *Wer hat dich, du schöner Wald* became standard repertoire of male choruses in Germany; Schumann's *Mondnacht*, *Zwielicht*, and *Frühlingsnacht* from the *Liederkreis*, Op. 39, are culmination points in the history of the *Lied*; Wolf's *Der Musikant* and *Seemanns Abschied*, which derive some pointed musical characteristics from Eichendorff's poetry, are almost as well known as Schumann's Eichendorff songs. In a list of the most popular poets of German songs (compiled by E. Challier in 1912), Eichendorff ranks sixth after Heine, Geibel, Hoffmann von Fallersleben, Goethe, and Uhland.[2] In a more recent study, Eckart Busse estimates the number of compositions based on Eichendorff texts in the nineteenth century to be over five thousand.[3]

Similar statistics are not yet available for the twentieth century. However, a cursory glance at various Eichendorff bibliographies and publishers' catalogs shows that Eichendorff's poems have continued to be a source of inspiration for many composers.[4] It is interesting to note that Eichendorff has been set in the twentieth century almost exclusively by composers not involved in the search for a radically new musical language (i.e., by composers such as Pfitzner, Schoeck, and Schwarz-Schilling, who may be considered late descendants of nineteenth-century Romanticism) or by composers, such as Christian Lahusen, Armin Knab, and Cesar Bresgen, who were closely associated with the musical youth movement in the 1920s.

The use of Eichendorff's lyrics for musical settings has not been restricted to composers of German-speaking countries. The popularity of the *Lied* spread to France, Scandinavia, Russia, and the United States in the nineteenth century and inspired developments there similar to those in Germany and Austria. In general, composers set lyrics of their native poets; but occasionally the non-Germanic composers also turned to the verses of Eichendorff, either in their original language or in translation, as a source of inspiration. Eichendorff was set, for instance, by the Bohemians Zdenko Fibich and A. M. Foerster, the Hungarian Emanuel Moór, the Alsatian V. E. Nessler, the French-Swiss E. Jaques-Dalcroze, the Dane Eduard Lassen, the Russian Nikolai Medtner, and the Americans Charles Converse and Louis Edgar Johns.

One might try to determine what attracted so many composers to Eichendorff's lyrics. Clearly, a composer is influenced in his choice of poetry by a variety of considerations, subjective as well as objective. On the one hand, special biographical circumstances may render a composer sympathetic to an emotional state expressed in a particular poem. Such motivation does not lend itself to generalization. On the other hand, structural aspects of the poetic imagery of the lyrics may make a poem suitable for a musical setting. These elements may be analyzed in order to discover, in part, what attracted composers to Eichendorff's poetry over and over again.

Folksong Qualities and Strophic Design

One of the chief reasons for the suitability of Eichendorff's poems to musical settings is their folksong-like character. Many of his lyrics are modeled after (or written against the background of) folk poetry. Eichendorff is deeply indebted to the anthology of folk poetry *Des Knaben Wunderhorn*, edited and published by Achim von Arnim and Clemens Brentano between 1806 and 1808.[5] This collection made a great impression on him and decisively shaped his thinking about poetry; actually, his earliest poems coincide approximately with the publication of the *Wunderhorn*. Eichendorff's lyrics resemble folk poetry in various respects, such as themes and imagery, diction and syntax, and strophic structure.[6]

The most representative example of such resemblance is the poem *Das zerbrochene Ringlein* (in this edition entitled *Untreue* [No. 1]). (All poems cited here to illustrate various details of Eichendorff's style are discussed in the Critical Notes.) The poem, written around 1810, elaborates the theme of unhappy love and echoes motives of the folksong *Müllers Abschied* from the *Wunderhorn* anthology. The present edition contains settings of several other poems in which Eichendorff absorbs themes and motives from folk poetry. *Waldgespräch* [No. 11], for example, is based on the ballad *Lore Lay* by Clemens Brentano, one of the editors of the *Wunderhorn*. This tale of the demonic seductress, probably invented by Brentano, was soon considered an authentic folk legend; it inspired, besides Eichendorff, Loeben and Heine ("Ich weiß nicht, was soll es bedeuten"). Eichendorff's poem may also have absorbed a Bohemian legend that features a riding forest-woman. The last stanza of his *Nachtlied* [No. 18] recalls motives from *Schall der Nacht*, which, although not an authentic folksong, found its way from Grimmelshausen's novel *Simplicissimus* of 1669 into the *Wunderhorn* anthology. The same poem reverberates as well in the first line of Eichendorff's *Der Einsiedler* [Nos. 2 and 7]. And the subject matter of *Die Kleine* [No. 9], for instance, is clearly based on the fourth stanza of *O Himmel was hab ich getan* from the *Wunderhorn*.

Eichendorff's poetic language is frequently characterized by a simplicity of diction that is ultimately derived from the folksong. Many features of *Das zerbrochene Ringlein*, for example, recall the language of folk poetry. The very beginning of the poem shows a syntactical figure typical of the folksong: the first strophe starts with the adverbial phrase "in einem kühlen Grunde," repeats it with the place-filler "da," and continues with verb and subject, grammatically the most important parts of the clause. This inverted construction can be found in many folksongs of the *Wunderhorn*. (It is also the model for the beginning lines of Eichendorff's *Die Kleine*.)

The popular vein of *Das zerbrochene Ringlein* is further underscored by apocopes deliberately used for metric reasons ("ich möcht'" instead of "ich möchte," "Treu" instead of "Treue"). The elisions of "ein'n" for "einen" and "blut'ge" for "blutige" are similar devices for avoiding an unwanted syllable. Where an unstressed syllable is needed, however, popular verse frequently inserts fillers such as "da," "und," and "wohl," or lengthens a verb by insertion of the vowel "e" ("gewohnet" instead of "gewohnt").

Yet another feature characteristic of popular verse that is apparent in Eichendorff is the looseness with which end-rhymes are treated in some cases. In *Das zerbrochene Ringlein* the rhyme "Grunde—verschwunden" in the first stanza is slightly impure because of the difference in the unstressed final syllables. In the last strophe, the pairing of first and third lines by means of end-rhymes is given up altogether. There the words "gehen" and "sterben" coincide only in the sound of the last stressed syllable, producing only a weak relationship. The missing rhyme in this case, however, is not simply a reflection of a folksong's typically casual approach to end-rhymes. It is, on the contrary, a well-calculated device that suggests the agony and stress of the lyric subject in the last strophe. (We shall return to this example later.) While elements of popular verse do appear in Eichendorff's poetry, they are, as the latter case shows, frequently handled in a refined way wholly different from the naiveté encountered in folksongs.[7]

The popular character of Eichendorff's poetry is revealed not only in the themes and motives treated in the poems nor just in the simplicity of diction that provides the poetic language, but also in the strophic forms in which the poet organizes his poems. The prevailing form of Eichendorff's poetry is the quatrain, a strophic pattern of four lines related to one another by an *abab* rhyme. It is a pattern that appears quite frequently in folk poetry, and Eichendorff seems to have favored this strophic form because of its simplicity and its qualities reminiscent of the folksong.

The composers represented in this edition also reveal this preference for the popular four-line strophe over all other patterns. The quatrain is the basic form for eight of the poems that inspired musical settings: *Das zerbrochene Ringlein* [No. 1], *Frühlingsnacht* [No. 3], *Der Morgen* [No. 10], *Waldgespräch* [No. 11], *Die Nachtblume* [No. 12], *In Danzig* [No. 17], *Nachtlied* [No. 18], and *Ergebung* [No. 19]. The eight-line strophes of *Am Strom* [No. 6], *Lockung* [No. 13], *Frische Fahrt* [No. 14], and *Marienlied* [No. 20] are simply extensions of the basic pattern by means of combining two quatrains. Further, the six-line strophes of *Die Kleine* [No. 9] can be reduced to quatrains, since the last two lines repeat material presented before. Five more settings are strophic. Hensel's and Kirchner's songs [Nos. 4 and 8] are based on the poem *Nachts* with the six-line stanza following an *aabccb* rhyme scheme. *Der Einsiedler* [Nos. 2 and 7] follows the same pattern. The poem *Abschied* [Nos. 5 and 16], which inspired both Franz and Pfitzner to settings, is based on a different six-line stanza rhyming *ababba*. The only setting based on a poem not organized in strophes is *Waldeinsamkeit* [No. 15].

Many nineteenth-century composers adhered, at least in their choice of poetry, to remnants of the song aesthetics of a former era. Before Schubert reshaped the genre of the *Lied* at the beginning of the century, a song was generally believed to be a composition based on a strophic text in which musical and poetic structure were closely related. Simple periodicity, four-measure phrase structure, relatively small ambitus, syllabic presentation of the text, and especially a strophic design were considered essential to the singable quality of the *Lied*. The concept of the *Lied* during the Goethe era was closely related to that of the folksong. Goethe and his contemporaries saw the folksong as something like a guiding star, something capable of preventing song composers from losing their bearings.[8]

Schubert, however, broke with the song aesthetics of the Goethe era by writing more elaborate piano accompaniments and by organizing his songs often in rather complex through-composed structures. By virtue of the variety and quality of his output, he set standards for the musical settings of poetry for several generations to come. As is well known, Goethe and his contemporaries did not approve of Schubert's courageous path, because they righteously clung to their understanding of the *Lied* as a genre related to the folksong.

Their view was reiterated in the nineteenth century by composers and aestheticians alike. Brahms, certainly a witness of some eminence, wrote to Clara Schumann in 1860: "The song is sailing now on such a wrong course that one cannot keep firmly enough in mind an ideal. And for me that is the folksong."[9] The philosopher Vischer, a descendant of Hegelian thought, stated in his *Aesthetics* of 1857: "The song is something that grows from nature; it can generate itself from life . . . therefore, the folksong is always the genuine source which purifies and refreshes the high art music of every epoch."[10] In other words: the simple strophic folksong was considered a corrective ideal to balance the diversifying forces that had gained prominence in the genre since Schubert.

Eichendorff's poems, as we have seen, have several features in common with the folksong and thus could be considered by many composers as a type of poetry supportive of their ideals. The strophic organization of Eichendorff's lyrics (in connection with the other aspects) is of major significance in accounting for their potential as *Lieder*. Although later generations did not have a concept of the *Lied* as limited as that held by poets and musicians before Schubert, it appears that the strophic design of the lyrics remained a strong factor throughout the nineteenth century in a composer's choice of poetry for musical settings. Whether they shared Brahms's nostalgia for the folksong, or whether they simply looked for a structural skeleton around which they could organize a composition (not necessarily resulting in a strophic musical design), composers seem to have been attracted to poems with a stanzaic organization.

Aural Imagery and Stimmung

Aside from the qualities that are reminiscent of folksongs, Eichendorff's poetry is characterized by other factors that make his verse particularly suited for musical settings. His poetic landscapes are communicated through images directed at the perception of the ear rather than that of other senses, and, thus, they lend themselves easily to musical transmutations. The singing of man and birds, the tones of various instruments, and the mysterious sounds of nature animate the landscapes that Eichendorff portrays in his lyrics.[11]

One of the acoustical images used most frequently is that of "rauschen" (rustling or murmuring). The word appears with an almost mannered consistency, connected with the sounds of forests, brooks, and springs. The rustling of trees and leaves or the murmuring of water symbolizes the musical potential of nature. It is, so to speak, music in its most elementary stage. That image often conveys the emotional states of quietude and peace of a nocturnal landscape (*Abschied* [Nos. 5 and 16]; *Der Einsiedler* [Nos. 2 and 7]), has a soothing quality (*Marienlied* [No. 20]), evokes melancholy memories (*Am Strom* [No. 6]), or lures the lyric subject into a magic world (*Lockung* [No. 13]). The rustling of the forest or the murmuring of streams is an irrational, unconscious expression of nature.

Musical instruments similarly animate the landscapes of Eichendorff's poems.[12] The instrument used more frequently than any other is the horn. In the baroque era the horn was a symbol of aristocratic entertainment; in Eichendorff's poems the horn suggests associations beyond those of hunting. Its sound confuses the senses with its uncertain, mysterious reverberations coming from changing directions (*Waldgespräch*, [No. 11]). The unpredictability of the horn calls suggests a confusion of emotions. Occasionally Eichendorff uses the image of the horn to express the longing of his heroes for traveling to remote places (*Frische Fahrt*, [No. 14]); in this function the hunting horn at other times is replaced by the posthorn, the image of which denotes distant travels and departures.

Likewise, musicians, instrumentalists, and singers frequently populate the landscapes of Eichendorff's poems. They are descendants of the medieval minstrels and goliards, wandering musicians who do not want to be integrated into society. Eichendorff's heroes are capable of spontaneous expression; they play their fiddles and pluck their lutes without embarrassment and sing whenever they feel like it. Music is the spontaneous expression of their joy and grief, their expectation and resignation (see *Der Morgen*, [No. 10]; *Frische Fahrt*, [No. 14]; *Der Einsiedler*, [Nos. 2 and 7]).

Musical features can be found in Eichendorff's lyrics not only in his poetic imagery but also in the poetic language itself. The sonorous aspect of the language—and this is true of Romantic poetry in general—becomes as important as the semantic aspect. Romantic poets, including Eichendorff, direct special attention to sonorous values of words and to the rhythmic-metric qualities of the verses. In many instances, Romantic poems are successful more because of their euphonious qualities than because of their semantic logic.[13]

The rhyme, especially the end-rhyme (as well as other correspondences of consonants and vowels), played a predominant role in the technique of exploiting the musical qualities of language in Romantic lyric poetry. The rhyme, a poetic tool that some eighteenth-century poets had considered abandoning altogether, enjoyed a general revival at the beginning of the nineteenth century. Most Romantic poets wrote in rhymed forms; unrhymed lyric poetry was the exception. In Eichendorff's poems the music of verbal sounds is not limited to end-rhymes. Correspondences between identical or similar consonants and vowels provide a web of sonorous relationships that can be used to mirror the emotional implications of a particular poetic situation.

The rhythmic-metric organization of a poem provides another layer of language—a "musical" layer as opposed to the semantic—that can be manipulated. Meter and declamation in a poem can either contradict or reinforce each other; they enter into varying degrees of conflict that can be manipulated according to the poem's content. Beyond this, end-stopped lines and enjambements establish larger time-units that can be related to one another in various ways so as to reflect the emotional situation depicted in the poetry.

Das zerbrochene Ringlein (*Untreue*, [No. 1]) may serve again as an example to clarify the manipulation of sonorous qualities in accordance with the poem's content. The emotional disturbance of the lyric subject is underscored by the abandonment of the end-rhyme in the last stanza. The regularity with which end-rhymes occur in the previous strophes of the poem builds up the reader's expectation that this regularity will continue. The expected similarity, however, is given up; the assimilation "gehen—sterben" interrupts the series of end-rhymes. The despair of the lyric subject is realized "musically" in the poetic language; an emotional nuance is conveyed by exploiting the sonorous quality of the words. Some rhythmic aspects in the same poem are also clearly related to its content. Enjambements in the third and fourth stanzas are used to depict the longing of the lyric subject to escape the agony of unrequited love by traveling into the world. End-stopped lines in the second and last stanzas serve as a means to depict rhythmically the destruction of the ring, as well as to portray the depressed psychological state of the poem's protagonist.

The musicalization of images and poetic language in Romantic lyrics is closely linked to the concept of *Stimmung*, which is at the core of the Romantic world view.[14] The term *Stimmung* in its original meaning refers to the way in which an instrument is tuned. Around the middle of the eighteenth century, probably under the influence of (or in connection with) the cultivation of sentiments in the era of *Empfindsamkeit*, the notion of "tuning" (*Stimmung*) began to be applied to the state of the human psyche. Since the 1770s, according to Paul Böckmann, *Stimmung* could refer to the disposition and inclination of the soul, and it is with the Romantic poets that these *Stimmungen* were made the deliberate objects of lyric poetry.[15]

The concept of *Stimmung*, though only vaguely definable, pervades Romantic thinking on art. When the Romantic poet speaks of the *Stimmung* of a landscape or an evening, he means both the atmosphere or "soul" condition of nature as manifested in that landscape or that evening and the impression these outside phenomena have made in the soul of the sympathetic observer. *Stimmung*, therefore, is the disposition of the soul when one is in a state of communication with something outside. In the state of *Stimmung*, one experiences an interrelationship between the self and nature: an outside phenomenon such as the nocturnal landscape reflects the disposition of the soul, or the soul corresponds harmoniously with the landscape.

Significantly, the term *Stimmung*, which is at the core of Eichendorff's concept of poetry, has musical origins. When Romantic artists use the term to describe the correspondence between outside world and lyric subject, the original meaning shines through. World and self are conceived as being in tune in such a way that the musics of the two correspond with one another. The music of the outside appearances blends with that of the soul in order to produce a *Stimmung*; the common link between the self and nature is music.

With this in mind, we can better understand the function of the many aural images in Eichendorff's poetry. The rustling of trees and the murmuring of brooks animate the landscapes; they lend to nature a soul that communicates with the self. For the Romantic poets, the rhyme is not only a structural device but, as Gillian Rodger has put it, "an audible means of conveying in lyric terms their ideal of universal harmony."[16] The rhyme relates different images to one another; the same function is served by the correspondences of verbal sound produced on the rhythmic-metric level.

Eichendorff's poetic style is not limited to the type of *Stimmungslyrik* just described (nor is he the only poet contributing to such lyrics). His poems include character portraits, often in the form of *Rollengedichte*; he handled the humorous rococo parody as well as he did the pensive-reflective sonnet. However, it was mostly through his nature lyrics that Eichendorff became a popular poet whose works were known and revered by people of all classes as part of a common cultural tradition. It was in his nature lyrics that Eichendorff popularized the "typical" Romantic forest landscape, in which springs and brooks murmur, trees rustle, nightingales sing of love, and memories of men go back in longing for the good old times. In ever-new constellations of images, Eichendorff tried to convey the correspondence between the self and nature known as *Stimmung*.

Composers throughout the nineteenth century were drawn to this type of poetry for their settings. Nature lyrics, more than any other type of poetry, attracted Schumann to Eichendorff's poems. For the twelve settings of his *Liederkreis*, Op. 39, as well as for four others, he mainly selected poems in which human emotional conditions mysteriously correspond to images of nature. The favorite scenic background of Schumann's settings is the nocturnal forest with its uncertain reverberating sounds and its vague rustling of treetops and leaves. Almost fifty years later, Hugo Wolf published his Eichendorff settings that explored a different aspect of the poet. While Wolf's volume still contains several songs of nature lyrics, the emphasis clearly rests upon more realistic and humorous themes, often those in which characters play roles (*Rollengedichte*); such poems enabled Wolf to compose markedly dramatic settings.

Most of the composers represented in this anthology show a clear preference for the tradition that Schumann's Eichendorff settings established. In fact, some of the poems included here were also set by Schumann (*Frühlingsnacht* [No. 3], *Waldgespräch* [No. 11], and *Der Einsiedler* [Nos. 2 and 7]), while many others are based on texts similar to those Schumann selected. Only *Die Kleine* [No. 9] is a *Rollengedicht* of the type preferred by Wolf. (Indeed, he set it to music in 1887; it was published posthumously in 1936.) The composers represented here show their indebtedness to the Schumannian model not only in their choice of poetry but also in the musical devices they employed in setting a poem. *Am Strom* [No. 6] by Franz, *Die Nachtblume* [No. 12] by Rheinberger, and *Abschied* [No. 16] by Pfitzner recall arpeggio-accompanied settings such as Schumann's *In der Fremde* (Op. 39, No. 1) or *Im wunderschönen Monat Mai* (Op. 48, No. 1); the piano part of Hopffer's *Lockung* [No. 13] is modeled after Schumann's *Schöne Fremde* (Op. 39, No. 6); the outdoor quality of Rudorff's *Frische Fahrt* [No. 14] can be found in several of Schumann's march-type wandering songs. It is only in the twentieth-century settings included here that the Schumann tradition is felt to a lesser extent.

Composers and Sources

FRIEDRICH GLÜCK composed one of the first and perhaps the most popular of all Eichendorff songs.[17] He was born September 23, 1793, in Oberensingen near Nütringen (Württemberg) as the first son of a minister. Like so many other young Swabians of great talent (Hegel, Hölderlin, Schelling), he was educated at the famous Gymnasium Stift in Tübingen, between 1809 and 1813. After a journey to Italy with which he capped his theological studies in 1814, he settled as a Protestant minister in Schorndorf (Württemberg). The responsibilities of a clergyman, however, seem to have been in conflict with the type of life he desired. He neglected his congregation and, thus, was often at odds with his superiors. Rather than fulfilling his duties, he socialized with army officers and artists. He enjoyed the friendship of the poet Lenau (among others) whose *Schilflieder* he set to music. Disappointed with his profession and unable to find a niche for his talent, he died embittered, on October 1, 1840.

His Eichendorff song *Untreue* ("In einem kühlen Grunde"), his most lasting contribution, was composed and published in 1814. The setting soon became part of the folk tradition. Friedrich Silcher's arrangement for male chorus further increased its popularity. Oral transmission, arrangements, and posthumous editions have produced numerous variants.

[1] *Untreue*. First edition: *Lieder / für eine Singstimme / mit Begleitung des Pianoforte / in Musik gesetzt / und seinem Freunde dem Herrn / Rittmeister von Vischer / gewidmet / von / Friedrich Glück / München bei Falter u. Sohn* [1814]. Copy in Deutsche Staatsbibliothek, Berlin (DDR), Musikabteilung, O. 77686. This copy carries an autograph dedication: "Dem Fräulein Binder vom Compositeur." The volume also contains settings of poems by Goethe and Uhland. Eichendorff is listed under his pen-name, Florens, which he used in his first publications.

JOSEPH DESSAUER was born on May 28, 1798, in Prague, where he studied piano and composition with Tomášek.[18] His frequent travels to Germany, Austria, France, England, and Italy brought him into contact with some of the greatest contemporary artists, who valued his friendship. Among his acquaintances were Bellini, Berlioz, Moscheles, Mendelssohn, Meyerbeer, and George Sand. From 1835 on, he had his residence in Vienna, interrupted by travels to various European resorts and spas during the summer months. The Vienna Society of the Friends of Music made him an honorary member in 1871 (perhaps in gratitude for an important copyist's score of Beethoven's *Eroica* that Dessauer purchased in 1827 and donated to the Society in 1870). He died in Mödling, near Vienna, on July 9, 1876.

[2] *Der Einsiedler*. Autograph manuscript: *Der Einsiedler / Gedicht von Joseph Freiherrn von Eichendorff / Musik von Jos. Dessauer / Herrn Anton Ritter von Pachner*. Deutsche Staatsbibliothek, Berlin (DDR), Musikabteilung, Mus. ms. autogr., Dessauer 1. As some markings concerning the disposition of pages and staves show in colored pencil, the manuscript was the source for the first edition of the song which has been consulted as a secondary source in the preparation of the present edition. First edition: *Der / Einsiedler / Gedicht / von Freih. von Eichendorff. / Musik von Joseph Dessauer. / . . . Wien bei H. F. Müller* [n.d.]. Plate number: H.F.M. 20.

FRIEDRICH CURSCHMANN was born on June 21, 1805, in Berlin, the son of a wine merchant.[19] After finishing school, he studied law in Berlin and Göttingen for a few years. His love for music made him decide in 1825 to become a composer; subsequently, he went to Kassel and studied with Spohr and Hauptmann. He returned to his hometown in 1829, where he stayed for the rest of his life (with the exception of a few travels to Paris and Vienna). Being independently wealthy, he was able to devote his life entirely to composition. During the 1830s he gained a following through performances of his songs in Berlin's bourgeois circles. Together with his wife, the soprano Rose Behrend, whom he married in 1837, he actively participated in the social and cultural life of Berlin. He died of appendicitis in 1841.

[3] *Frühlingsnacht, Op. 20, No. 4*. First collected edition [?]: *Curschmann-Album. / Sämtliche / Lieder und Gesänge / für eine / Singstimme mit Begleitung des Piano-*

forte / componirt von / Fr. Curschmann . . . Berlin: Schlesinger [1871]. Copy in Sibley Music Library, Eastman School of Music, Rochester, New York.

FANNY HENSEL, Felix Mendelssohn's older sister, was born in Hamburg on November 14, 1805.[20] A few years later, the family moved to Berlin, where she received a thorough general and musical education. Trained by Ludwig Berger, she became an excellent pianist and performed frequently during the "Sonntagsmusiken" in her parents' house. After her brother's departure from home, she directed these private concerts for the rest of her life. In 1829 she married the court painter Wilhelm Hensel (1794–1861), with whom she had a son, Sebastian (1830–98). During the 1830s and 1840s, the Mendelssohn-Hensel household was one of the centers of Berlin's cultural life, mainly because of her social and artistic efforts. A stroke during a rehearsal of Mendelssohn's *Walpurgisnacht* led to her premature death on May 14, 1847.

According to Krautwurst, Fanny Hensel was undoubtedly the most important woman composer of the nineteenth century. Although she began to compose at an early age, publication of her works was not considered for a long time. Some of her songs were printed among the works of her brother Felix. Only at the end of her life (and posthumously) were any of Fanny Hensel's works published under her own name: songs, songs-without-words, and a piano trio. Both her last composition, the song *O Lust vom Berg zu schauen*, and her brother's final work, *Nachtlied* ("Vergangen ist der lichte Tag") of 1847, are Eichendorff settings.

[4] *Nachtwanderer, Op. 7, No. 1*. First edition: *Sechs / Lieder / für eine Stimme mit Begleitung des Pianoforte / componirt und ihre Schwester / Frau / R. Lejeune Dirichlet / zugeeignet von / Fanny Hensel / . . .* Berlin and Breslau: Bote & Bock [1846]. Plate number: 1050. Copy in Library of Congress, Washington, D.C., Music Division. (I am grateful to Dr. Carol L. Quin of Lane College, Jackson, Tennessee, for calling the first edition to my attention.) The autograph copy in the Nydahl Collection of the Stiftelsen Musikkulturens främjande (Stockholm) was consulted as a secondary source. This autograph copy contains the following dedication at the end of the song: "Zu freundlichem Andenken für Fräulein Auguste Löwe. Berlin, Dec. 1846. Fanny Hensel."

ROBERT FRANZ, one of the most prolific composers of songs in the nineteenth century, was born in Halle on June 28, 1815, and died there on October 24, 1892.[21] His parents were slow to recognize the musical talent of their son; not until the age of twenty was he allowed to study composition, which he did with Friedrich Schneider in Dessau. After his return to Halle in 1837, he served his hometown for the remainder of his life as organist, choral conductor, and director of music at the university. Because of approaching deafness and nervous disorders, he was forced to resign his posts in 1867. Generous gifts from friends helped him through ensuing financial difficulties.

Franz devoted his creativity almost exclusively to the composition of about 350 solo songs with piano accompaniment, most of them on texts by Heine and Wilhelm Osterwald. His first set of *Lieder* was favorably reviewed by Schumann in 1843; subsequently he gained the admiration and respect of other nineteenth-century composers, including Mendelssohn, Gade, and Liszt.

[5] *Abends, Op. 16, No. 4*. Early edition: Robert Franz. *Sechs Gesänge, Op. 16*. Leipzig: Siegel [ca. 1865]. Plate number: 1659. Copy in Library of Congress, Washington, D.C., Music Division. The songs are dedicated to "Ihrer Königlichen Hoheit Sophie, Erb-Großherzogin zu Sachsen, geb. Prinzessin der Niederlande."

[6] *Am Strom, Op. 30, No. 3*. Early edition: Robert Franz. *Sechs Lieder, Op. 30*. Leipzig: Kistner [1857]. Plate number: 2267, 4100. Copy in Library of Congress, Washington, D.C., Music Division.

KARL REINTHALER was born on October 13, 1822, in Erfurt.[22] He studied theology and music in Berlin (the latter with A. B. Marx). Supported by a royal stipend, he traveled to Paris and Italy in 1849 to continue his musical education for three years. On his return he taught at the conservatory in Cologne. In 1857 he became organist and conductor in Bremen, a post he retained until his retirement in 1887. Reinthaler was a staunch supporter of Brahms, and one of the highlights of his career came when he conducted the first performance of Brahms's *Deutsches Requiem* in 1868. An extensive correspondence between the two men documents their friendship. Reinthaler died on February 13, 1896, in Bremen.

Reinthaler was active as a composer of several operas, a symphony, choral works (often sacred), and songs. His greatest success was his oratorio *Jephtha*.

[7] *Der Einsiedler*. Autograph manuscript: *Der Einsiedler v. Eichendorff*. Deutsche Staatsbibliothek, Berlin (DDR), Musikabteilung, Mus. ms. autogr., Reinthaler 1. At the end of the song, there is an autograph dedication: "K. Reinthaler seinem Waldgen."

THEODOR KIRCHNER was born on December 10, 1823, in Neukirchen near Chemnitz (today Karl-Marx-Stadt).[23] His musical talent was developed at an early age through piano and organ lessons. As a young man he moved to Leipzig, where he continued his musical education with Julius Knorr and C. F. Becker; in 1843 he enrolled as the first student in the newly founded Leipzig Conservatory. Schumann and Mendelssohn respected his musicianship and furthered his career. On the latter's recommendation he became organist in Winterthur, a post he held until 1862. During these years he developed an active concert life in Winterthur and also toured Germany as a keyboard player. In Zürich (his residence until 1872), he conducted the orchestra and a chorus. Realizing that he was not successful as a conductor, he limited his activities after a few years to organ and piano playing, especially as accompanist of the singer Julius Stockhausen. Brahms became his good friend during this time. In his next position as director of the new conservatory in Würzburg, he felt uncomfortable; when his eccentric way of life created problems for him, he resigned from this responsibility in 1876. In the following years he lived in Leipzig and Dresden as a composer and teacher, frequently in financial difficulties. In 1890 he moved to Hamburg where he died on September 18, 1903.

Kirchner devoted his creative talent mainly to the composition of small-scale works. With his character pieces for piano and songs, he continued the Mendelssohn-Schumann tradition for almost fifty years beyond the death of its originators.

[8] *Ich wandre durch die stille Nacht, Op. 95*. Early, possibly first, edition: Theodor Kirchner, *Ich wandre durch die stille Nacht für eine Singstimme mit Begleitung des Pianoforte, Op. 95*. Greiz: Willy von Franquet [ca. 1890]. Plate number: 224. Copy in Library of Congress, Washington, D.C., Music Division.

FRANZ VON HOLSTEIN was born on February 16, 1826, in Brunswick, into an age-old aristocratic family.[24] Despite artistic inclinations, he was obliged to pursue a military career. Nevertheless, supported by his mother's family in Wolfenbüttel and by Robert Griepenkerl, who taught at the military academy in Brunswick, the young Holstein was able to undertake musical studies in his spare time. A first opera was written while he was preparing for the officer's examination; another one originated shortly after he returned from the Schleswig-Holstein campaign of 1848/49. In 1853 he finally decided to quit his military career and to study with Moscheles and Hauptmann at the Leipzig Conservatory. The Dresden performance of his opera *Der Haideschacht* in 1868 was undoubtedly the culmination of his activities as a poet-composer. His other operas were not as successful. After the death of Moritz Hauptmann in 1868, Holstein became the president of the Bach Gesellschaft. Exhausted from his various activites and weakened by a long history of nervous disorders, he died on May 22, 1878, in Leipzig. For many years after his death, a Holstein Foundation provided a haven for needy students of the Leipzig Conservatory.

[9] *Die Kleine, Op. 37, No. 1*. First collected edition [?]: *39 / Lieder und Gesänge / für eine / Singstimme / mit Begleitung des Pianoforte / komponirt / von / Franz von Holstein*. Leipzig: Breitkopf & Härtel [1884]. Plate number: V.A. 495. Copy in New York Public Library, Performing Arts Research Center.

EDUARD LASSEN was born in Copenhagen on April 13, 1830.[25] After a musical education at the conservatory in Brussels, Lassen received several awards that allowed him to tour other countries and seek contact with leading European artists. During his travels to Germany and Italy, he met Spohr and Liszt. The successful premiere of one of Lassen's operas in Weimar with Liszt as conductor led to a position as music director in that city in 1857. A year later he succeeded Liszt as court music director. Supported by friends such as Liszt, Bülow, and Cornelius, he remained in this position until his retirement in 1895. The performance of Wagner's *Tristan* in 1875 under his baton marked the high point of his career as a conductor. He died in Weimar on January 15, 1904.

[10] *Der Morgen, Op. 81, No. 3*. Probably first edition: Eduard Lassen. *Sechs Lieder, Op. 81*. Breslau: Julius Hainauer [n.d.]. Plate number: J2852H. Copy in Library of Congress, Washington, D.C., Music Division.

ADOLF JENSEN was born into a family of talented musicians on January 12, 1837, in Königsberg (today Kaliningrad).[26] Mainly self-taught, he eventually held various positions in Grodno (Russia), Posen (Poznań), and Copenhagen, where his career was furthered by Niels Gade. After several years he returned to Königsberg as a conductor, teacher, and pianist. The musical life of his hometown flourished under his guidance. During these years (1860 to 1866) he encouraged performances of works by Wagner and Liszt, among others. Jensen then briefly settled in Berlin as a piano pedagogue. The last ten years of his life saw him in constant search of a climate that would help overcome the tuberculosis from which he never recovered. Dresden, Merano, Graz, and Baden-Baden were his last residences. He died in Baden-Baden on January 23, 1879.

Jensen composed mainly piano music, choral works, and songs, most of them in Königsberg during the 1860s, which were years of relatively good health for him. In style, his compositions are a late manifestation of Schumannian Romanticism.

[11] *Waldesgespräch, Op. 5, No. 4*. First edition: *Vier Gesänge / (nach Poesien von Georg Herwegh und Eichendorff) / für eine / Singstimme / mit Begleitung des Pianoforte / componirt von / Adolf Jensen Op. 5*. Hamburg: Fritz Schuberth [1861]. Plate number: 558. Copy in New York Public Library, Performing Arts Research Center.

JOSEPH RHEINBERGER was born on March 17, 1839, in Vaduz, the capital of the small principality of Liechtenstein.[27] The musical talent of the child was recognized early by his parents and furthered through private lessons. In 1851 he moved to Munich, which remained his residence for the rest of his life; here he also met teachers who developed his compositional and instrumental skills. He soon found employment as a theory and piano teacher and as an organist at a number of churches. In 1867, he became a professor at the conservatory—a post he held until his retirement. He died on November 25, 1901, in Munich.

Throughout his life, Rheinberger composed in various vocal and instrumental genres, especially sacred music and works for organ. He achieved his most lasting fame as a well-known and much sought-after teacher (Humperdinck, Wolf-Ferrari, Sandberger, and Kroyer were among his students). His reputation even attracted musicians from the other side of the Atlantic Ocean such as the Americans Horatio Parker and G. W. Chadwick. Rheinberger received many honors at the end of his life.

[12] *Die Nachtblume, Op. 22, No. 2*. First edition: Josef Rheinberger. *Vier Gesänge, Op. 22*. Leipzig: E. W. Fritzsch [ca. 1861]. Plate number: 7375. Copy in Library of Congress, Washington, D.C., Music Division. The songs are dedicated to "Frl. Sophie Stehle."

BERNHARD HOPFFER was born on August 7, 1840, in Berlin, the son of a goldsmith and jeweler.[28] After finishing school, he studied composition at the Kullak Academy of Music in Berlin until 1860. In his twenties he composed an opera *Frithjof* (first performed in Berlin in 1871), several symphonies, cantatas, chamber music, and songs. Because of a lung condition, he was forced to live in spas in Italy and Switzerland between 1872 and 1876. As much as his health permitted, he continued to pursue his ambitions as a composer. Hopffer was deeply depressed when his brother Emil died of tuberculosis in the summer of 1877 in Wiesbaden; a few weeks later, on August 20, 1877, the disease claimed him too as a victim. He died in a resort near Rüdesheim.

[13] *Lockung, Op. 22, No. 1*. Autograph manuscript: *[3 Lieder by Eichendorff, Heyse, and Platen]*. Deutsche Staatsbibliothek, Berlin (DDR), Musikabteilung, Mus. ms. autogr., B. Hopffer 80. *Lockung* is dated "27. 1. [18]72." The other two songs in the manuscript are *Mädchenlied* and *Klagelied Ottos III*. *Lockung* was published as Op. 22, No. 1, by Schlesinger in Berlin. Plate number: 7033.

ERNST RUDORFF was born on January 18, 1840, in Berlin and died there on December 31, 1916.[29] He began studying theology and philosophy in Berlin in 1859 but soon moved to Leipzig, where he could add music to his curriculum. Moscheles, Reinecke, and Hauptmann were his teachers at the Leipzig Conservatory. After four years as pianist and choral conductor in Cologne (1865 to 1869), he became the first piano professor at the Berlin Hochschule für Musik, a post that he held until his retirement in 1910. Between 1880 and 1890 he succeeded Max Bruch as director of the Stern *Gesangverein*, one of Berlin's most distinguished singing societies. He composed in a variety of genres: overtures and symphonies, choral works, chamber music, compositions for piano, and songs. After his retirement he devoted his activities to the idea of environmental protection (*Naturschutz*).

[14] *Frische Fahrt, Op. 16, No. 2*. Autograph manuscript: *Vier Lieder / für Singstimme mit Begleitung des Pianoforte / componirt / von / Ernst Rudorff / Op. 16 / Julius Janitzsch / Zugeeignet*. Deutsche Staatsbibliothek, Berlin (DDR), Musikabteilung, Mus. ms. autogr., E. Rudorff 12. The first edition was consulted as a secondary source: *Vier Lieder / für eine Singstimme / mit Begleitung des Pianoforte / componirt / von / Ernst Rudorff* . . . Berlin & Posen: Bote & Bock [n.d.]. Plate number: 10387.

PHILIPP SPITTA, known primarily as a Bach biographer, was born on December 7, 1841, in Wechold near Hoya (Lower Saxony).[30] Despite a great musical talent, he decided, in 1860, to study classical languages at the University of Göttingen. After completing his dissertation on the Roman historian Tacitus in 1864, he became a teacher of Latin and Greek in Reval (today Tallinn, in Estonia), Sondershausen, and Leipzig. In 1875—the first volume of his Bach biography had appeared meanwhile—he accepted a position as professor of music history in Berlin; at the same time he became administrative director of the Hochschule für Musik. He had a tremendous impact on the development of musicology; Max Seiffert, Adolf Sandberger, Max Friedlaender, Peter Wagner, and Johannes Wolf, among others, were his students. Exhausted from his various activities, Spitta died from a heart attack on April 13, 1894.

Spitta composed only in his youth, although various chamber works and songs reveal some extraordinary compositional talent that could have been developed further. According to his nephew Heinrich Spitta, a meeting with Brahms in Göttingen may have led Spitta to abandon composition in favor of a philological career.

[15] *Waldeinsamkeit*. Autograph manuscript: *Acht Lieder von Eichendorff / für eine Singstimme mit Pianoforte-Begleitung / componiert von / Philipp Spitta / (im Sommer 1860)*. Deutsche Staatsbibliothek, Berlin (DDR), Musikabteilung, Mus. ms. autogr., Ph. Spitta 5. The song in the present edition, *Waldeinsamkeit*, is the second of the cycle. The others are: 1) *Gute Nacht*, 3) *In der Fremde* ("Aus der Heimat"), 4) *Frühlingsgruß*, 5) *Nachts* ("Hörst du die Gründe rufen"), 6) *Vom Berge*, 7) *Mondnacht* and 8) *Waldessehnsucht*.

HANS PFITZNER was born into a family of musicians in Moscow on May 5, 1869.[31] His compositional talent was soon recognized and developed at the conservatory in Frankfurt, where his parents had moved in 1872. When he left the conservatory in 1890, he had already written a number of substantial works. The following years saw him as conductor and teacher of composition in various locations, Berlin and Munich, among others. In 1899 he married the daughter of James Kwast, his former piano teacher, by eloping with her to Canterbury. Before he accepted a position as conductor of the symphony orchestra (later also of the opera) in Straßburg in 1908, he had written three operas that were premiered around the turn of the century in various German cities. The years in Straßburg were the most fruitful of his life. Besides working there as stage director, conductor, and author, he composed his main opus, the opera *Palestrina* (premiered in Munich in 1917). At the end of World War I, he moved to Munich. Beginning in 1920, he taught master classes in composition for the Berlin Academy of the Arts and, after 1929, at the Munich Academy as well. He remained active as a composer of orchestral music, chamber works, and vocal music to the end of his life. He died in Salzburg on May 22, 1949, shortly after his eightieth birthday.

The poems of Eichendorff were the backbone of Pfitzner's song settings. Between 1888 and 1931 he wrote nineteen songs on Eichendorff texts. The two songs published here are representative of his early and middle periods, respectively.

[16] *Abschied, Op. 9, No. 5*. First edition: Hans Pfitzner. *Fünf Lieder nach Gedichten von Eichendorff, Op. 9*. Leipzig: Brockhaus [1898]. Plate number: M.B. 335. Copy owned by the present editor. The songs were composed in 1888/89 and dedicated to Anton Sistermans. Reprinted by permission of Max Brockhaus, Musikverlag, 53 Bonn 2, Germany. All rights reserved.

[17] *In Danzig, Op. 22, No. 1*. First edition: Hans Pfitzner. *Fünf Lieder, Op. 22*. Leipzig: Brockhaus [1907]. Plate number: M.B. 536. Copy owned by the present editor. Reprinted with permission of Max Brockhaus, Musikverlag, 53 Bonn 2, Germany. All rights reserved.

OTHMAR SCHOECK was born into an artistic family on September 1, 1886, in Brunnen (Schwyz).[32] Following in the footsteps of his father, he first inclined toward the visual arts, but soon music became his principal calling. He attended the Zurich conservatory and in 1907/08 studied briefly with Reger in Leipzig. He returned to Zurich to become conductor of various choral societies; from 1917 to 1944 he conducted the symphony orchestra in St. Gallen (without, however, giving up his residence in Zurich). He found another outlet for his aspirations as a performer by accompanying various instrumentalists and singers. Throughout his life, he composed songs, operas, chamber works, and orchestral music. A heart attack in 1944 forced Schoeck to curtail his activities as a conductor. Having received many honors in the last decade of his life, he died on March 8, 1957, in Zurich.

Schoeck was one of the principal composers of songs in the first half of the twentieth century. Like Pfitzner, he considered the lyrics of Eichendorff particularly well-suited to musical settings. Between 1907 and 1952, he composed over fifty songs after poems by Eichendorff.

[18] *Nachtlied, Op. 20, No. 13*. First edition: Othmar Schoeck. *Lieder nach Gedichten von Eichendorff und Uhland für eine Singstimme und Klavier, Op. 20*. Leipzig: Breitkopf & Härtel [1917]. Plate number: E.B. 5026 (27984). Copy in Staatsbibliothek Preußischer Kulturbesitz, Berlin (West), Musikabteilung. Plate number: 187063. The song was composed in October 1914 in Zurich. Reprinted by permission of Breitkopf & Härtel, Wiesbaden, Germany.

[19] *Ergebung, Op. 30, No. 6*. First edition: Othmar Schoeck. *Zwölf Eichendorff-Lieder für eine Singstimme und Klavier, Op. 30*. Leipzig: Breitkopf & Härtel, 1921. Plate number: E.B. 5201–04 (28682). Copy in Deutsche Staatsbibliothek, Berlin (DDR), Musikabteilung, 190681. The song was composed on October 7, 1918, in Brunnen. Reprinted by permission of Breitkopf & Härtel, Wiesbaden, Germany.

REINHARD SCHWARZ-SCHILLING was born on May 9, 1904, in Hanover.[33] He studied music (composition, conducting, piano, and organ) in Munich, Florence, and Cologne with Walter Braunfels, Philipp Jarnach, and Heinrich Kaminski. After some years as a freelance artist, choir director, and organ teacher in Innsbruck, he became a professor of composition at the Berlin Hochschule für Musik, where he headed the composition department for a few years before his retirement in 1971. He has toured extensively in Europe, North America, and South Korea as conductor, organist, and pianist. His creativity has been directed primarily to the composition of vocal music (mostly sacred) and orchestral and chamber works. He presently lives in Berlin-Grunewald.

[20] *Marienlied*. First edition: Reinhard Schwarz-Schilling. *Drei Lieder nach Gedichten von Joseph von Eichendorff für Bariton (Alt) und Klavier*. Kassel: Bärenreiter, 1949. Plate number: 2144. Copy owned by the present editor. *Marienlied*, the second of three Eichendorff songs, is dedicated to the memory of Hermann Töpfers, a Catholic clergyman who died in a Nazi labor camp. The other two songs are *Todeslust* and *Kurze Fahrt*. Reprinted by permission of Bärenreiter-Verlag, Kassel, Germany.

Critical Commentary

The sources for the twenty songs published in the present edition were compiled from the holdings of various European and American libraries: Deutsche Staatsbibliothek (Berlin, DDR), Staatsbibliothek Preußischer Kulturbesitz (Berlin-West), New York Public Library, Library of Congress (Washington, D.C.), Sibley Music Library (Rochester, N.Y.), and the Nydahl Collection (Stockholm). Autographs or first editions were given preference as sources for the edition. In a few cases, however, early editions had to suffice. This occurred when autographs and first editions were unavailable or when, especially in the case of minor composers, the current state of research does not permit us to distinguish with any certainty which early edition is the first. In truth, it may make little difference to the musical text, because the plates from the first edition are frequently used unchanged for subsequent publications.

A "one-source" method was used for editing the songs: if both autograph and first edition were available, as was the case with a few songs, the former served as the principal source, while the latter was consulted as a secondary source. This policy was reversed only for Fanny Hensel's *Nachtwanderer* [No. 4], because the Stockholm autograph appeared to be a hastily written copy of the song (probably intended as a gift) and not quite suited to serve here as a principal source.

By and large, the variants between the sources and the present edition are minor and do not affect the compositional substance. Editorial revision includes regularization of inconsistent styling among the various printers and autographs when such styling does not affect the musical interpretation. In the case of autographs, especially of unpublished songs, the editor frequently had to correct obvious errors. The changes occur mostly in the realm of dynamics and articulation; alterations of pitches and durational values are rare. Dynamic markings and rests supplied by the editor in one part on the basis of indications present in the other part have been enclosed in brackets and are not reported in the critical notes. The same procedure was followed when dynamic markings and rests were added on the basis of analogies to parallel passages. Those cautionary accidentals in the source deemed unnecessary by the editor have been removed without comment. All editorial accidentals, including editorially prescribed cautionary accidentals, are in brackets. In summary, beyond these principles all editorial additions of any type that are not bracketed are listed in the critical notes.

The poems underlaid in the music are left essentially as they appear in the source. However, spellings and punctuation have been modernized in approximate conformity with the practice of the critical edition of Eichendorff's works (hereafter called HKA).[34] In a few cases, the composer's text differs considerably from the poet's version; for comparison, the latter has been printed in all cases in the Critical Commentary. The prose translations of the poems, provided in parentheses by the editor, do not aspire to communicate any of the poetic subtleties of the text; they are intended instead to give the reader and performer a first understanding of the poem at a quick glance.

The critical commentary for the individual songs is organized as follows: a) the poem taken from *HKA*, b) a prose translation of the poem, c) comments on the poem with references to sources on the textual history of the poem (from *HKA* as well as the Eichendorff commentary by Hillach and Krabiel, hereafter called *EK*),[35] d) notes on the text, and e) notes on the music.

The notes on the text report differences in the composer's version of the poem as compared with the *HKA*. The notes on the music describe the source consulted when it is at variance with the edition. Abbreviations used are as follows: v. = voice; p. = piano; rh = right hand of piano part; lh = left hand of piano part. Pitches are given according to the Helmholtz system wherein c' = middle C, c'' = the C above middle C, and so forth.

[1] *Untreue* (Glück)

Das zerbrochene Ringlein

In einem kühlen Grunde
Da geht ein Mühlenrad,
Mein' Liebste ist verschwunden,
Die dort gewohnt hat.

Sie hat mir Treu' versprochen,
Gab mir ein'n Ring dabei,
Sie hat die Treu' gebrochen,
Mein Ringlein sprang entzwei.

Ich möcht' als Spielmann reisen
Weit in die Welt hinaus,
Und singen meine Weisen,
Und gehn von Haus zu Haus.

Ich möcht' als Reiter fliegen
Wohl in die blut'ge Schlacht,
Um stille Feuer liegen
Im Feld bei dunkler Nacht.

Hör' ich das Mühlrad gehen:
Ich weiß nicht, was ich will—
Ich möcht' am liebsten sterben,
Da wär's auf einmal still!

(In a cool vale turns a mill-wheel. My love who lived there has vanished.

She pledged me her faith, gave me a ring. She broke her vow; the ring broke in two.

I'd like to travel as a minstrel far into the world and sing my songs from door to door.

I'd like to rush into a bloody battle as a knight, to lie around quiet fires at night in the field.

Whenever I hear the mill-wheel turning, I feel at a loss. I wish I could die; then at last all would be still.)

Text in *HKA* I/1, p. 438. The poem was first published under the title *Lied* in the almanac *Deutscher Dichterwald*, ed. Justinus Kerner, Friedrich de la Motte-Fouqué, Ludwig Uhland, and others. Tübingen: 1813. This must undoubtedly have been the textual source for Glück's setting (in later editions the title is *Das zerbrochene Ringlein*). (See *HKA* I/2, pp. 786–91, and *EK* I, pp. 79–80.)

TEXT: Title is *Untreue* instead of *Das zerbrochene Ringlein*. Strophe 1, line 3, "Liebchen" instead of "Liebste." Strophe 1, line 4, "Das" instead of "Die."

MUSIC: M. 1, p., *p* below note 3. M. 3, p., *p* between notes 3 and 4. Mm. 3, 4, 7, 8, p., slurs from cue-size notes to main note are lacking. M. 9, p., crescendo only up to note 5. M. 11, p., slurs from cue-size notes to main note are lacking.

[2] *Der Einsiedler* (Dessauer)

Der Einsiedler

Komm, Trost der Welt, du stille Nacht!
Wie steigst du von den Bergen sacht,

Die Lüfte alle schlafen,
Ein Schiffer nur noch wandermüd',
Singt übers Meer sein Abendlied
Zu Gottes Lob im Hafen.

Die Jahre wie die Wolken gehn
Und lassen mich hier einsam stehn,
Die Welt hat mich vergessen,
Da trat'st du wunderbar zu mir,
Wenn ich beim Waldesrauschen hier
Gedankenvoll gesessen.

O Trost der Welt, du stille Nacht!
Der Tag hat mich so müd' gemacht,
Das weite Meer schon dunkelt,
Laß ausruhn mich von Lust und Not,
Bis daß das ew'ge Morgenrot
Den stillen Wald durchfunkelt.

(Come, silent night, comfort of the world; how gently you descend from the mountains. All breezes sleep; only a sailor in the harbor, tired of wandering, sings his evening song across the sea, in praise of God.

The years pass by like clouds and leave me standing here alone; the world has forgotten me; and then you came so wonderfully to me as I sat here, lost in thought in the shadow of the woods.

O silent night, comfort of the world, the day has left me so tired. Darkness creeps over the wide sea. Now let me rest from pleasure and pain until the sunrise of eternity penetrates the silent forest.)

Text in *HKA* I/1, p. 372. The poem was first published in the 1837 edition of Eichendorff's collected poems and in *Deutscher Musenalmanach* (1837) ed. by Adalbert von Chamisso. Eichendorff used the poem also as a lyric insertion in his novella *Eine Meerfahrt* (posthumously published in 1864). (See *HKA* I/2, p. 766, and *EK* I, p. 75.)

TEXT: Strophe 3, line 5, "einst" instead of "daß." (The word "daß" is crossed out in the autograph and replaced by "einst.")

MUSIC: M. 15, p.lh, note 2 lacks staccato—edition follows the first edition. M. 16, v., crescendo only to beginning of measure; note 3 is marked *ff*—edition follows the first edition. M. 38, p.lh, crescendo only to note 4.

[3] *Frühlingsnacht* (Curschmann)

Frühlingsnacht

Über'n Garten durch die Lüfte
Hört' ich Wandervögel ziehn,
Das bedeutet Frühlingsdüfte,
Unten fängt's schon an zu blühn.

Jauchzen möcht' ich, möchte weinen,
Ist mir's doch, als könnt's nicht sein!
Alte Wunder wieder scheinen
Mit dem Mondesglanz herein.

Und der Mond, die Sterne sagen's.
Und in Träumen rauscht's der Hain,
Und die Nachtigallen schlagen's:
Sie ist Deine, sie ist dein!

(Above the garden in the air I heard migrant birds flying; that tells of fragrances of spring; below, it already begins to bloom.

I want to rejoice, I want to cry; it seems as if it cannot be true. Old miracles glow again in the moonlight.

And moon and stars say it, the grove rustles it in dreams, and the nightingales sing it: She is yours, is yours.)

Text in *HKA* I/1, p. 280. The poem was first published in the 1837 edition of Eichendorff's collected poems. (See *HKA* I/2, p. 739, and *EK* I, p. 69).

[4] *Nachtwanderer* (Hensel)

Nachts

Ich wandre durch die stille Nacht,
Da schleicht der Mond so heimlich sacht
Oft aus der dunklen Wolkenhülle,
Und hin und her im Tal
Erwacht die Nachtigall,
Dann wieder alles grau und stille.

O wunderbarer Nachtgesang:
Von fern im Land der Ströme Gang,
Leis Schauern in den dunklen Bäumen—
Wirrst die Gedanken mir,
Mein irres Singen hier
Ist wie ein Rufen nur aus Träumen.

(As I wander through the silent night, often glides the moon so gently from behind the dark clouds. Here and there in the valley awakens the nightingale. Then once more all is grey and still.

O wonderful song of the night: from afar in the country the sound of streams, a light shiver in the dark trees—you confound my thoughts. My confused singing here is like a call out of dreams.)

Text in *HKA* I/1, p. 8. The poem was first published in the appendix to Eichendorff's novellas *Taugenichts* and *Marmorbild* in 1826. It appeared there as the first of five poems forming the lyric cycle *Nachtbilder*. In the 1837 edition of Eichendorff's collected poems, "Ich wandre durch die stille Nacht" and another one of the cycle were published under the title *Nachtwanderer*. In the 1841 edition of Eichendorff's works, the cycle was completely dissolved and the poem under consideration was titled *Nachts*. Since Fanny Hensel retained the heading *Nachtwanderer* for her setting, it is obvious that she used the 1837 edition as a textual source. (See *HKA* I/2, p. 642, and *EK* I, p. 49.)

TEXT: Strophe 1, line 3, "dunkeln" instead of "dunklen." Strophe 2, line 3, "dunkeln" instead of "dunklen." Strophe 2, line 4, "irrst" instead of "wirrst." Strophe 2, line 5, "wirres" instead of "irres."

MUSIC: Mm. 5–6, 12, p., pedal and end-of-pedal markings are lacking—edition follows autograph. M. 19, p., crescendo begins at note 7—edition follows autograph. M. 26, p., tremolos are erroneously notated: 4 thirty-second-notes plus a tremolo of a half-note add up to a 5/8 meter—adjusted to the prevailing 6/8 meter. M. 27, p., end-of-pedal marking at end of measure—edition follows autograph. M. 28, p., tremolo erroneously notated: 4 thirty-second-notes plus a tremolo of a half-note add up to a 5/8 meter—adjusted to the prevailing 6/8 meter. M. 29, p., no end-of-pedal marking—edition follows autograph. M. 30, p., tremolo erroneously notated: 4 thirty-second-notes plus a tremolo of a half-note add up to a 5/8 meter—adjusted to the prevailing 6/8 meter; no pedal marking—edition follows autograph; p.rh, accent added by analogy with mm. 26 and 28. M. 32, v., dotted half-note only—edition follows autograph. M. 37, p.lh, note 2 is C dotted quarter-note—edition follows autograph.

[5] *Abends* (Franz)

Abschied

Abendlich schon rauscht der Wald
Aus den tiefen Gründen,
Droben wird der Herr nun bald
An die Sterne zünden,
Wie so stille in den Schlünden,
Abendlich nur rauscht der Wald.

Alles geht zu seiner Ruh',
Wald und Welt versausen,
Schauernd hört der Wandrer zu,
Sehnt sich recht nach Hause,
Hier in Waldes grüner Klause
Herz, geh endlich auch zur Ruh'!

(In the evening rustles the forest out of the depth. Up above, the Lord will soon light the stars. How quietly rustles the forest in the depths in the evening.

All goes to rest; forest and world fade away. Shivering, the wanderer listens and yearns to be home. Here in the forest's green cloister, heart, you, too, go to rest.)

Text in *HKA* I/1, p. 381. The poem was first published in the 1837 edition of Eichendorff's collected poems. (See *HKA* I/2, p. 768 and *EK* I, p. 75.)

TEXT: Title is *Abends* instead of *Abschied*. Strophe 1, line 2, "tiefsten" instead of "tiefen." Strophe 1, line 4, "Bald die Stern' anzünden" instead of "An die Sterne zünden." Strophe 1, line 5, "Gründen" instead of "Schlünden." Strophe 2, line 4, "wohl" instead of "recht." Strophe 2, line 6, insertion of "du" between "endlich" and "auch." The extra syllable supports the ritardando; the additional rhyme "du-Ruh" increases the concluding effect.

MUSIC: M. 6, p., no pedal ending. M. 8, p., decrescendo up to note 8. M. 9, p.lh, no slur over the whole measure—added by analogy with m. 1. M. 13, p., crescendo up to note 4. M. 14, v., p., crescendo up to note 6.

[6] *Am Strom* (Franz)

Am Strom

Der Fluß glitt einsam hin und rauschte,
Wie sonst, noch immer, immerfort,
Ich stand am Strand gelehnt und lauschte,
Ach, was ich liebt', war lange fort!
Kein Laut, kein Windeshauch, kein Singen
Ging durch den weiten Mittag schwül,
Verträumt die stillen Weiden hingen
Hinab bis in die Wellen kühl.

Die waren alle wie Sirenen
Mit feuchtem, langem, grünem Haar,
Und von der alten Zeit voll Sehnen
Sie sangen leis und wunderbar.
Sing, Weide, singe, grüne Weide!
Wie Stimmen aus der Liebsten Grab
Zieht mich dein heimlich Lied voll Leide
Zum Strom von Wehmut mit hinab.

(The river flowed on in solitude and murmured, ever as before. I stood on the bank and listened. Alas, what I loved left long ago! No sound, no breeze, no singing moved through the great, oppressive noon. Dreaming, the silent willows hung down into the cool waves.

They all were like sirens with wet, long, green hair and full of longing from ancient times. Their song was soft and wonderful. Sing, willow, sing, green willow! Like sounds from the grave of my beloved, your secret song of pain draws me down into the stream of melancholy.)

Text in *HKA* I/1, p. 316. The poem was first published in the 1837 edition of Eichendorff's collected poems. (See *HKA* I/2, pp. 748–49, and *EK* I, p. 71.)

TEXT: Strophe 1, line 1, "Strom" instead of "Fluß." Strophe 1, line 4, "liebte" instead of "liebt." Strophe 2, line 3, "Ach" instead of "Und."

MUSIC: M. 3, p., decrescendo only to note 3; v., crescendo only to note 7. Mm. 3, 6, p.rh, notes 5, 9, and 13 are eighth-notes. M. 10, p.rh, note 1 quarter-note a-sharp is lacking. Mm. 18, 21, p.rh, notes 5, 9, and 13 are eighth-notes. M. 25, v., crescendo begins between notes 3 and 4 and ends between notes 5 and 6. M. 26, v., decrescendo ends between notes 1 and 2. M. 27, v., crescendo only to note 2.

[7] *Der Einsiedler* (Reinthaler)

For text and translation of the poem, see Joseph Dessauer's *Der Einsiedler* [No. 2].

TEXT: Strophe 3, line 2, "trüb" instead of "müd."

Music: The manuscript contains the following pedal markings: *Ped* (M. 8, between notes 1 and 2); end of *Ped* (M. 9, note 5); *Ped* (M. 16, note 6); *Ped* (M. 45, between notes 2 and 3); end of *Ped* (M. 46, note 5); *Ped* (M. 54, between notes 4 and 5). The composer was apparently very inconsistent in notating the pedal. Edition deletes all pedal markings and replaces them with the prescription *mit Pedal* at the beginning of the song. M. 4, p.rh, slur is lacking. Mm. 6–8, p.rh, slur only for m. 6. Mm. 8–9 and 9–10, p.rh, slurs lacking from second chord to first chord of next measure. M. 12, p.lh, note 1 is not only c but also C—eliminated by analogy with m. 49. Mm. 12–13, p.lh, slur only from notes 2 to 4—editorially emended by analogy with m. 14. Mm. 14–15, p.lh, slur only to note 4 of m. 14. M. 18, p.rh, note 1 is e'. M. 21, p.rh, note 4 is f'. M. 22, p., slurs from second quarter-note to beginning of m. 23 are lacking—added by analogy with preceding measures. M. 39, p.lh, note 7 is B' also as quarter-note—deleted as unnecessary. Mm. 39–40, p.rh, lacks slur. M. 40, p.rh, lacks slur from notes 2 to 3. M. 41, p.rh, lacks slur. M. 47, p.rh, slur from notes 2 to 3—eliminated by analogy with m. 10. M. 53, p.rh, lacks slur.

[8] *Ich wandre durch die stille Nacht* (Kirchner)

For text and translation of the poem, see Fanny Hensel's *Nachtwanderer* [No. 4].

Text: The first line of the poem becomes the title of the song.

Music: Mm. 10, 17, 29, p., crescendo only to end of measure.

[9] *Die Kleine* (von Holstein)

Die Kleine

Zwischen Bergen, liebe Mutter,
Weit den Wald entlang,
Reiten da drei junge Jäger
Auf drei Rößlein blank,
 lieb' Mutter,
Auf drei Rößlein blank.

Ihr könnt fröhlich sein, lieb' Mutter
Wird es draußen still:
Kommt der Vater heim vom Walde,
Küßt Euch, wie er will.
 lieb' Mutter,
Küßt Euch, wie er will.

Und *ich* werfe mich im Bettchen
Nachts ohn' Unterlaß,
Kehr' mich links und kehr' mich rechts hin,
Nirgends hab' ich was,
 lieb' Mutter,
Nirgends hab' ich was.

Bin ich eine Frau erst einmal,
In der Nacht dann still
Wend' ich mich nach allen Seiten,
Küß, soviel ich will,
 lieb' Mutter,
Küß, soviel ich will.

(Between the mountains, dear mother, along the wide wood, ride three young hunters on three little horses, dear mother, on three little horses.

You can be happy, dear mother, when it gets quiet outside, father comes home from the forest and kisses you as he wishes, dear mother, and kisses you as he wishes.

And I toss around on the bed, restlessly all night, turn left, turn right, and have nothing, dear mother, and have nothing.

Once I am a woman, during the night I will quietly turn to all sides, kiss as much as I wish, dear mother, kiss as much as I wish.)

Text in *HKA* I/1, p. 250. The poem was first published as a lyric insertion in the novel *Ahnung und Gegenwart* of 1815. In the appendix of the edition of *Taugenichts* and *Marmorbild* of 1826, it appears under the title *Die Fröhliche*. The title was changed to *Die Kleine* in the 1837 edition of Eichendorff's collected poems. (See *HKA* I/2, p. 731, and *EK* I, p. 68.)

Text: Holstein, who wrote the librettos of his own operas, replaced the third and fourth strophes of Eichendorff's poem with two from his own pen in this setting.

Seltsam Bangen mir im Herzen
Pocht ohn' Unterlaß,
Oft von heißen Sehnsuchtstränen
Wird mein Kissen naß,
 lieb' Mutter,
Wird mein Kissen naß.

Bin ich eine Frau erst einmal,
Wird es draußen still,
Halt' den Liebsten ich umschlungen,
Küß so viel ich will,
 lieb' Mutter,
Küß so viel ich will.

(Strange anguish beats in my heart without ceasing; from hot tears of longing, often my pillow is wet, dear mother, my pillow is wet.

Once I am a woman, when it gets quiet outside, I will hold my lover tightly, kiss as much as I wish, dear mother, kiss as much as I wish.)

Music: M. 14, p., crescendo only leading up to note 3. Mm. 17–18, p.lh, lacks slur for lower voice. Mm. 19–20, p.rh, lacks slur for upper voice. M. 20, p., crescendo only leading up to note 2. M. 25, p.lh, note 1 lacks staccato mark. M. 29, p., note 1 lacks staccato marks.

[10] *Der Morgen* (Lassen)

Der Morgen

Fliegt der erste Morgenstrahl
Durch das stille Nebeltal,
Rauscht erwachend Wald und Hügel:
Wer da fliegen kann, nimmt Flügel!

Und sein Hütlein in die Luft
Wirft der Mensch vor Lust und ruft:
Hat Gesang doch auch noch Schwingen,
Nun, so will ich fröhlich singen!

Hinaus, o Mensch, weit in die Welt,
Bangt dir das Herz in krankem Mut;
Nichts ist so trüb in Nacht gestellt,
Der Morgen leicht macht's wieder gut.

(When the first morning ray flies through the quiet foggy valley, forests and hills awaken and rustle. Whoever can fly takes wing.

Rejoicing, man throws his cap into the air and shouts: "Since songs also have wings, I will sing cheerfully!"

If your spirits are low, O man, go forth into the world. Nothing is so dreary and dark that the fresh morning cannot heal it again.)

Text in *HKA* I/1, p. 35. Strophes 1 and 2 of the poem were first published in 1826 as lyric insertions of the novella *Aus dem Leben eines Taugenichts*; strophe 3 appeared first as a lyric insertion in the novel *Ahnung und Gegenwart* of 1815. The three strophes were published under the title *Der Morgen* in the 1837 edition of Eichendorff's poems. (See *HKA* I/2, p. 654, and *EK* I, p. 52.)

[11] *Waldesgespräch* (Jensen)

Waldgespräch

Es ist schon spät, es wird schon kalt,
Was reit'st du einsam durch den Wald?
Der Wald ist lang, du bist allein,
Du schöne Braut! Ich führ' dich heim!

"Groß ist der Männer Trug und List,
Vor Schmerz mein Herz gebrochen ist,
Wohl irrt das Waldhorn her und hin,
O flieh! Du weißt nicht, wer ich bin."

So reich geschmückt ist Roß and Weib,
So wunderschön der junge Leib,
Jetzt kenn' ich dich—Gott steh' mir bei!
Du bist die Hexe Lorelei.

"Du kennst mich wohl—von hohem Stein
Schaut still mein Schloß tief in den Rhein.
Es ist schon spät, es wird schon kalt,
Kommst nimmermehr aus diesem Wald!"

(It is late and growing cold; why are you riding alone through the woods? The woods are long, you are alone. Fair lady, let me lead you home.

Great is the cunning and the deceit of men; my heart breaks with pain. The hunting horn wanders here and there; flee, you know not who I am.

So richly adorned are steed and lady, so exquisite the young figure—now I know you, God be with me—you are the witch Lorelei!

You know me well. From the towering rock my castle gazes silently deep into the Rhine. It is late and growing cold; you never shall leave these woods again.)

Text in *HKA* I/1, p. 431. The poem was first published as a lyric insertion in the novel *Ahnung und Gegenwart* of 1815; it appeared independently in the 1837 edition of Eichendorff's collected poems. (See *HKA* I/2, p. 784, and *EK* I, pp. 78–79.)

TEXT: Except for the title, there are no textual changes. It is possible that Jensen followed Schumann (*Liederkreis*, Op. 39, No. 3) in altering the title from *Waldgespräch* to *Waldesgespräch*. Both Schumann and Jensen returned unknowingly to an original intention of the poet (see Hilde Schulhof, "Zur Textgeschicte von Eichendorffs Gedichten," *Zeitschrift für deutsche Philologie*, Vol. 47 [1918], p. 70). In order to prepare for the ghostly character of his setting, Jensen prefaced the song with a poetic motto by an unidentified author: "The midnight wind howls, hoarse and gloomy, like whispers from the graves of the dead."

MUSIC: Mm. 6–7, 10–11, 29–30, v., crescendo only to end of m. 6 (m. 10 or m. 29, respectively); decrescendo begins on note 1 of m. 7 (m. 11 or m. 30, respectively); p., crescendo only to end of m. 6 (m. 10, m. 29, respectively). Mm. 18–19, v., p., crescendo only to end of m. 18. Mm. 49–50, p., crescendo only to end of m. 49.

[12] *Die Nachtblume* (Rheinberger)

Die Nachtblume

Nacht ist wie ein stilles Meer,
Lust und Leid und Liebesklagen
Kommen so verworren her
In dem linden Wellenschlagen.

Wünsche wie die Wolken sind,
Schiffen durch die stillen Räume,
Wer erkennt im lauen Wind,
Ob's Gedanken oder Träume?—

Schließ' ich nun auch Herz und Mund,
Die so gern den Sternen klagen:
Leise doch im Herzensgrund
Bleibt das linde Wellenschlagen.

(Night is like the silent sea; joy, sorrow, and love's lament sound so confusing in the soft splashing of the waves.

Wishes are like clouds—they move through quiet spaces. Who knows in the gentle wind whether they are thoughts or dreams?

I close now my heart and lips, which like so much to confess to the stars, but deep in my heart lingers the soft splashing of the waves.)

Text in *HKA* I/1, p. 261. The poem was first published in the 1837 edition of Eichendorff's collected poems. It is contained in the manuscript version of *Dichter und ihre Gesellen* and, therefore, must have been written in the early 1830s. (See *HKA* I/2, p. 734, and *EK* I, p. 67.)

Text: Strophe 2, line 2, "leeren" instead of "stillen."

Music: M. 8, v., crescendo only up to end of measure. Mm. 16, 19–25, p.rh, crescendo-decrescendo pair begins on note 12 and is centered on end of measure—editorially emended by analogy with other measures. M. 28, v., crescendo only up to end of measure. Mm. 31, 33–35, p.rh, crescendo-descresendo pair begins on note 12 and is centered on end of measure—editorially emended by analogy with other measures.

[13] *Lockung* (Hopffer)

Lockung

Hörst du nicht die Bäume rauschen
Draußen durch die stille Rund'?
Lockt's dich nicht, hinabzulauschen
Von dem Söller in den Grund,
Wo die vielen Bäche gehen
Wunderbar im Mondenschein
Und die stillen Schlösser sehen
In den Fluß vom hohen Stein?

Kennst du noch die irren Lieder
Aus der alten, schönen Zeit?
Sie erwachen alle wieder
Nachts in Waldeseinsamkeit,
Wenn die Bäume träumend lauschen
Und der Flieder duftet schwül
Und im Fluß die Nixen rauschen—
Komm herab, hier ist's so kühl.

(Don't you hear the treetops rustle from the silent field outside? Aren't you tempted to listen down from the heights into the chasm where many brooks flow, wonderful in the moonlight, and quiet castles gaze from rocks above into the river?

Do you still know the strange songs of the good old days? They all awaken again at night in the solitude of the forest, when the trees listen dreamily and the lilacs breathe their heavy fragrance and the nymphs play in the river—come down, here it is so cool.)

Text in *HKA* I/1, p. 112. The poem was first published as a lyric insertion in the novel *Dichter und ihre Gesellen* of 1834. It appeared independently in the 1837 edition of Eichendorff's collected poems. (See *HKA* I/2, p. 683, and *EK* I, p. 58.)

[14] *Frische Fahrt* (Rudorff)

Frische Fahrt

Laue Luft kommt blau geflossen,
Frühling, Frühling soll es sein!
Waldwärts Hörnerklang geschossen,
Mut'ger Augen lichter Schein;
Und das Wirren bunt und bunter
Wird ein magisch wilder Fluß,
In die schöne Welt hinunter
Lockt dich dieses Stromes Gruß.

Und ich mag mich nicht bewahren!
Weit von euch treibt mich der Wind,
Auf dem Strome will ich fahren,
Von dem Glanze selig blind!
Tausend Stimmen lockend schlagen,
Hoch Aurora flammend weht,
Fahre zu! Ich mag nicht fragen,
Wo die Fahrt zu Ende geht!

(Mild air comes flowing; spring, it must be spring! The sound of horns, the sparkle of eyes turn toward the woods. And crowds, growing more and more colorful, become a magic, wild flow. The greetings of this stream lure me out into the beautiful world.

I do not want to stay behind. The wind will drive me far from you. Blissful, blinded by the light, I want to travel on the stream. A thousand voices lure me on, the flaming banner of Aurora waves on high. Farewell, I dare not ask where this journey will end!)

Text in *HKA* I/1, p. 3. The poem was first published as a lyric insertion in the novel *Ahnung und Gegenwart* (1815). (See *HKA* I/2, p. 639, and *EK* I, p. 49).

Music: M. 31, p.rh, ties for e' and c' are lacking—edition follows first edition and by analogy to m. 10.

[15] *Waldeinsamkeit* (Spitta)

Waldeinsamkeit!
Du grünes Revier,
Wie liegt so weit
Die Welt von hier!
Schlaf nur, wie bald
Kommt der Abend schön,
Durch den stillen Wald
Die Quellen gehn,
Die Mutter Gottes wacht,
Mit ihrem Sternenkleid
Bedeckt sie dich sacht
In der Waldeinsamkeit,
Gute Nacht, gute Nacht!—

(Solitude of the forest, you green grove! How distant is the world from here. Sleep, how soon comes the beautiful evening, when the springs flow through the silent forest and the Mother of God wakes, protecting you with her starry dress in the solitude of the forest. Good night, good night!)

Text in *HKA* I/1, p. 365. The poem was first published as a lyric insertion in the novel *Dichter und ihre Gesellen* of 1834; in the 1837 edition of Eichendorff's poems, it appeared as the fifth poem of the poetic cycle *Der Umkehrende*. (See *HKA* I/2, pp. 764–65, and *EK* I, p. 74.)

TEXT: The first line of the poem becomes the title of the song.

MUSIC: M. 17, p.lh, lacks slur from notes 1 to 2. M. 19, v., slur added from note 3 to m. 20, note 2. M. 23, v., slur extended to m. 24, note 2. M. 30, p., crescendo only to end of measure.

[16] *Abschied* (Pfitzner)

For text and translation of the poem, see Robert Franz's *Abends* [No. 5].

MUSIC: M. 8, p.rh, d' (in middle voice) is half-note—editorially emended by analogy with m. 5. M. 18ff., p.lh, slurs appear to be part of the quadruplet and octuplet marks. However, by analogy to the first strophe (mm. 1–17), they may also be understood as slurs indicating legato playing. M. 21, p.lh, legato slur for notes 1 to 3 is lacking (see preceding remark). M. 26, p.lh, legato slurs for notes 1 to 4 are lacking in both voices—editorially emended by analogy with m. 11. Mm. 26–28, p.lh, two slurs from notes 1 to 6 in mm. 27 and 28—articulation marks editorially emended by analogy with mm. 12–13.

[17] *In Danzig* (Pfitzner)

In Danzig (1842)

Dunkle Giebel, hohe Fenster,
Türme tief aus Nebeln sehn,
Bleiche Statuen wie Gespenster
Lautlos an den Türen stehn.

Träumerisch der Mond drauf scheinet,
Dem die Stadt gar wohl gefällt,
Als läg zauberhaft versteinet
Drunten eine Märchenwelt.

Ringsher durch das tiefe Lauschen,
Über alle Häuser weit,
Nur des Meeres fernes Rauschen—
Wunderbare Einsamkeit!

Und der Türmer wie vor Jahren
Singet ein uraltes Lied:
Wolle Gott den Schiffer wahren,
Der bei Nacht vorüberzieht!

(Dark roofs, high windows, and towers emerge from the depth of the mist. Pale statues stand silently like phantoms at the doors.

Well pleased by the town, the moon shines dreamily on it as if down there lay a fairy-tale world, magically turned to stone.

All around the deep silence above all houses: only the distant murmur of the ocean—wonderful solitude!

And the watchman as for many years sings an age-old song: May God protect the sailor who passes by at night!)

Text in Joseph von Eichendorff, *Sämtliche Gedichte*, ed. Wolfdietrich Rasch (Munich: Deutscher Taschenbuch Verlag, 1975), p. 425. The poem was first published posthumously in the second edition of Eichendorff's collected works in 1864, prepared by his son Hermann von Eichendorff, who titled the poem *In Danzig* and dated it 1842. The original title was probably *Nachts (Danzig 1843)*. (See *EK* I, p. 97.)

MUSIC: M. 35, p.rh, note 1 is b'-flat eighth-note—editorially emended by analogy with m. 34. M. 37, p.rh, g' (dotted quarter-note) tied to g' in m. 36 is lacking. M. 41, p.rh, g' (quarter-note) and tie to g' in m. 40 are lacking—editorially emended by analogy with m. 37. M. 59, p.lh, slur added from grace-note.

[18] *Nachtlied* (Schoeck)

Nachtlied

Vergangen ist der lichte Tag,
Von ferne kommt der Glocken Schlag;
So reist die Zeit die ganze Nacht,
Nimmt manchen mit, der's nicht gedacht.

Wo ist nun hin die bunte Lust,
Des Freundes Trost and treue Brust,
Des Weibes süßer Augenschein?
Will keiner mit mir munter sein?

Da's nun so stille auf der Welt,
Ziehn Wolken einsam übers Feld,
Und Feld und Baum besprechen sich,—
O Menschenkind! was schauert dich?

Wie weit die falsche Welt auch sei,
Bleibt mir doch Einer nur getreu,
Der mit mir weint, der mit mir wacht,
Wenn ich nur recht an ihn gedacht.

Frisch auf denn, liebe Nachtigall,
Du Wasserfall mit hellem Schall!
Gott loben wollen wir vereint,
Bis daß der lichte Morgen scheint!

(The bright day is passed. From afar comes the tolling of the bell. So travels time the whole night long, takes with it some who never knew.

Where is now the pleasure of the day, the solace and loyal heart of friends, the sweet sparkle of a maiden's eyes? Will no one be awake with me?

It is now so still on earth, lonely clouds pass over the field, and field and tree converse. O child of man, why are you shivering?

However false the world may be, if only one stays faithful who weeps with me, who wakes with me when I think of him.

Come on, dear nightingale, and your waterfall with clear sound. Let us praise God together until the bright morning breaks.)

Text in *HKA* I/1, p. 384. The poem was first published as a lyric insertion in the novel *Ahnung und Gegenwart* (1815). In the appendix to the 1826 edition of the novellas *Taugenichts* and *Marmorbild*, it appeared as part of the lyric cycle *Nachtbilder*. It was published as an independent poem in the 1837 edition of Eichendorff's collected poems. (See *HKA* I/2, p. 768, and *EK* I, p. 75.)

MUSIC: M. 33, p.rh, no tie from note 4(c') to note 7(c'). M. 58, crescendo to end of measure.

[19] *Ergebung* (Schoeck)

Ergebung

Es wandelt, was wir schauen,
Tag sinkt ins Abendrot,
Die Lust hat eignes Grauen,
Und alles hat den Tod.

Ins Leben schleicht das Leiden
Sich heimlich wie ein Dieb,
Wir alle müssen scheiden
Von allem, was uns lieb.

Was gäb' es doch auf Erden,
Wer hielt' den Jammer aus,
Wer möcht' geboren werden,
Hielt'st Du nicht droben Haus!

Du bist's, der, was wir bauen,
Mild über uns zerbricht,
Daß wir den Himmel schauen—
Darum so klag' ich nicht.

(All we see are changes. Day sinks into sunset. Pleasure has its own terror and all ends in death.

Suffering creeps into life secretly like a thief. We all must part from everything we love.

What would matter on earth, who could tolerate the misery, who would want to be born—if you did not live above.

It is you above who shatters what we build here on earth so that we should see heaven. That's why I do not complain.)

Text in *HKA* I/1, p. 365. The poem was first published in the 1837 edition of Eichendorff's collected poems as a part of the lyric cycle *Der Umkehrende* (see also *Waldeinsamkeit* [No. 15] by Spitta). In the second edition of Eichendorff's works of 1864, prepared by the poet's son Hermann von Eichendorff, the poem appears as an independent unit under the title *Ergebung*. This edition or a later one derived from the 1864 edition was undoubtedly the textual source for Schoeck's setting. (See *HKA* I/2, pp. 764–65, and *EK* I, p. 74.)

MUSIC: Mm. 2, 3, 4, p., crescendo only up to note 5—editorially emended by analogy with m. 1. M. 6, v., crescendo only to note 4. M. 8, v., p., crescendo only to end of measure. M. 13, p.rh, staccato mark on note 4—portato sign added by analogy with preceding measures. M. 18, p., crescendo only to note 4—editorially emended by analogy with earlier measures. M. 19, p., crescendo only to end of measure—editorially emended for contextual considerations. M. 23, p., decrescendo begins at note 8—editorially emended by analogy with other measures. M. 24, p., crescendo only to end of measure—editorially emended for contextual considerations.

[20] *Marienlied* (Schwarz-Schilling)

Marienlied

Wenn ins Land die Wetter hängen
Und der Mensch erschrocken steht,
Wendet, wie mit Glockenklängen,
Die Gewitter Dein Gebet,
Und wo aus den grauen Wogen
Weinend auftaucht das Gefild,
Segnest Du's vom Regenbogen—
Mutter, ach, wie bist Du mild!

Wenn's einst dunkelt auf den Gipfeln
Und der kühle Abend sacht
Niederrauschet in den Wipfeln:
O Maria, heil'ge Nacht!
Laß mich nimmer wie die andern,
Decke zu der letzten Ruh'
Mütterlich den müden Wandrer
Mit dem Sternenmantel zu.

(When thunderstorms hang in the air and man stands frightened, your prayer, as if with sounds of chimes, turns away the tempest. And where, from the heavy rains, the field emerges in tears, you bless it from the rainbow. Mother, oh, how kind you are!

When it gets dark on the mountains and the cool evening softly whispers down onto the treetops. Oh, Mary, holy night! Never leave me like the others. As a mother, cover the tired wanderer with a mantle of stars for his final rest.)

Text in *HKA* I/1, p. 403. The poem was first published in the first edition of Eichendorff's collected works in 1841. (See *HKA* I/2, p. 775, and *EK* I, p. 76.)

Acknowledgments

I wish to acknowledge the support of the following individuals in the preparation of the edition: Dr. Wolfgang Goldhan (Berlin), Dr. Peter Hug-Ricklin (Zürich), Dr. Hans Joachim Klein (Berlin), Dr. Karlheinz Köhler (Weimar, formerly Berlin), Dr. Erling Lomnäs (Stockholm), Dr. Carol L. Quin (Jackson, Tennessee), Mr. Joachim von Roebel (Bonn), Ms. Mary Wolinsky (Waltham, Massachusetts, formerly Rochester), Mr. Walter Zuochenko (New York). Special thanks go to Ms. Jean Harden (Ithaca) and the late Dr. Jerald C. Graue for valuable suggestions during the editorial process and proofreading of the manuscript.

February 1983

Jurgen Thym
Eastman School of Music
Rochester, N.Y.

Notes

1. For a detailed discussion of Eichendorff's impact on the German people and the political implications, see Eberhard Lämmert, "Eichendorffs Wandel unter den Deutschen: Überlegungen zur Wirkungsgeschichte seiner Dichtung," in *Die deutsche Romantik*, ed. Hans Steffen (2nd edition; Göttingen: Vandenhoek & Ruprecht, 1970), pp. 219–252.

2. Ernst Challier, "Die Lieblingsdichter der Deutschen," *Das Literarische Echo* 15 (1912–1913): 359. The list is reprinted as Appendix III in Jessie H. Kneisel, *Mörike and Music* (Ph.D. diss., Columbia University, 1949), pp. 208–210.

3. Eckart Busse, *Die Eichendorff-Rezeption im Kunstlied* (Würzburg: Eichendorff-Gesellschaft, 1975), p. 9.

4. Settings by twentieth-century composers are listed in the "Eichendorff-Bibliographie" of the Eichendorff-Gesellschaft's yearbook, *Aurora*, vol. 13ff. (1953 and subsequent years). Karl Freiherr von Eichendorff, *Ein Jahrhundert Eichendorff-Literatur* (Regensburg: Habbel, 1924), does not list settings of Eichendorff poems.

5. Eichendorff studied in the academic year 1807/08 at the University of Heidelberg. The editors of the *Wunderhorn* had resided there for several years and, though they had since left the city, their ideas were still current in the academic community. Joseph von Görres, a close associate of Arnim and Brentano, became Eichendorff's most influential teacher during this time. Eichendorff came into personal contact with the editors of the *Wunderhorn* some years later in Berlin. In his autobiographical essay "Halle und Heidelberg" (Joseph Freiherr von Eichendorff, *Aus dem literarischen Nachlasse*, Paderborn: Schöningh, 1866; pp. 290–329) he portrays very vividly the circle of philosophers and artists who made Heidelberg the center of late literary Romanticism during those years.

6. For a detailed discussion of the relationships between folksong and Eichendorff's poetry, see Jacob Harold Heinzelmann, *The Influence of the German Volkslied on Eichendorff's Lyric* (Leipzig: Fock, 1910). The study was originally written as a Ph.D. dissertation at the University of Chicago.

7. See also Paul Salmon, "Romanticism and the German Language," in *The Romantic Period in Germany*, ed. S. S. Prawer (London: Weidenfeld and Nicolson, 1970), pp. 235–258, particularly pp. 240–244.

8. See Heinrich W. Schwab, *Sangbarkeit, Popularität und Kunstlied: Studien zu Lied und Liedästhetik der mittleren Goethezeit 1770–1814* (Regensburg: Bosse, 1965); and Heinrich Jaskola, "Vom Geheimnis des Liedes: Theoretische Erwägungen Goethes und der Seinen zur Wort- und Tonkunst des Liedes," *Aurora* 26 (1966): 66–81.

9. Clara Schumann—Johannes Brahms, *Briefe*, ed. Berthold Litzmann, vol. I (Leipzig: Breitkopf und Härtel, 1927), p. 294. ("Das Lied segelt jetzt so falschen Kurs, daß man sich ein Ideal nicht fest genug einprägen kann. Und das ist mir das Volkslied.")

10. As quoted in Walter Wiora, *Das deutsche Lied: Zur Geschichte und Ästhetik einer musikalischen Gattung* (Wolfenbüttel and Zurich: Möseler, 1971), p. 15. ("Das Lied ist etwas Naturwüchsiges, das aus dem Leben selbst sich erzeugen kann. . . . daher das Volkslied stets die reine Quelle bleibt, aus welcher auch der höhern Tonkunst jedes Zeitalters stets neue Läuterung und Erfrischung zuströmt.")

11. See René Wehrli, *Eichendorffs Erlebnis und Gestaltung der Sinnenwelt* (Leipzig: Huber, 1938); Otto Friedrich Bollnow, "Das romantische Weltbild bei Eichendorff," in *Unruhe und Geborgenheit im Weltbild neuerer Dichter* by O. F. Bollnow (Stuttgart: Kohlhammer, 1953), pp. 227–259; and Heinz Hillmann, *Bildlichkeit der deutschen Romantik* (Frankfurt/Main: Athenäum, 1971), particularly pp. 220–222. See also Hans Joachim Moser, "Eichendorff und die Musik," in *Musik in Zeit und Raum* by H. J. Moser (Berlin: Merseburger, 1961), pp. 205–220.

12. For a detailed discussion, see Erich Worbs, "Waldhornruf und Lautenklang: Musikinstrumente in der Dichtung Eichendorffs," *Aurora* 22 (1962): 74–81.

13. This is particularly true for the poems of Ludwig Tieck and for some of Clemens Brentano. See Johannes Mittenzwei, *Das Musikalische in der Literatur* (Halle: VEB Verlag Sprache und Literatur, 1962), pp. 112–118 and 143–161, respectively.

14. Emil Staiger, "Dichtung und Musik in der Romantik," *Universitas* 4 (1949): 1057–1064. See also Hans Jürg Lüthi, *Dichtung und Dichter bei Joseph von Eichendorff* (Bern and Munich: Francke, 1966).

15. Paul Böckmann, "Formen der Stimmungslyrik," in *Formensprache* by Paul Böckmann (Darmstadt: Wissenschaftliche Buchgesellschaft, 1969). For a detailed discussion of the changes in the concept of *Stimmung*, see: Richard Erny, "Sprachmusikalität als ästhetisches Problem der Vorromantik," *Jahrbuch der deutschen Schillergesellschaft* 2 (Stuttgart: Kröner, 1958): 114–144.

16. Gillian Rodger, "The Lyric," in *The Romantic Period in Germany*, ed. Prawer, p. 168.

17. Karl Otto Frey, "Friedrich Glück: Ein grosser Unbekannter," *Aurora* 13 (1953): 53–55.

18. *MGG*, s.v. "Joseph Dessauer," by Karl Pfannhauser.

19. *MGG*, s.v. "Karl Friedrich Curschmann," by Willi Kahl; G. Meissner, "Karl Friedrich Curschmann. Ein Beitrag zur Geschichte des deutschen Liedes zu Anfang des 19. Jahrhunderts" (Phil. Diss., University of Leipzig, 1899); Hans Hermann Rosenwald, *Geschichte des deutschen Liedes zwischen Schubert und Schumann* (Berlin: Edition Benno Balan, 1930), pp. 82–84.

20. Sebastian Hensel, *Die Familie Mendelssohn 1729–1847* (Berlin: B. Behr, 1879); *MGG*, s.v. "Fanny Hensel," by Franz Krautwurst; Eric Werner, *Mendelssohn* (London: Collier-MacMillan, 1963).

21. *MGG*, s.v. "Robert Franz," by Walter Serauky.

22. *MGG*, s.v. "Karl Reinthaler," by Reinhold Sietz.

23. Reinhold Sietz, *Theodor Kirchner: Ein Klaviermeister der deutschen Romantik*, Studien zur Musikgeschichte des 19. Jahrhunderts, vol. 21 (Regensburg: Bosse, 1971); *MGG*, s.v. "Theodor Kirchner," by Reinhold Sietz.

24. *MGG*, s.v. "Franz von Holstein," by Willi Kahl; G. Glaser, "Franz von Holstein: Ein Dichterkomponist des 19. Jahrhunderts" (Phil. Diss., Leipzig, 1930).

25. *MGG*, s.v. "Eduard Lassen," by Günther Kraft; Magda Marx-Weber, "Die Lieder Eduard Lassens," *Hamburger Jahrbuch für Musikwissenschaft* 2 (Hamburg: Wagner, 1980).

26. *MGG*, s.v. "Adolf Jensen," by Reinhold Sietz.

27. *MGG*, s.v. "Joseph Gabriel Rheinberger," by Anton Würz.

28. *Allgemeine Deutsche Biographie* XIII (Leipzig: Duncker & Humblot, 1881), pp. 105–06.

29. *MGG*, s.v. "Ernst Rudorff," by Imogen Fellinger; Nancy B. Reich, "The Rudorff Collection," *Notes* 31 (1975): 247–61; Ernst Rudorff, *Aus den Tagen der Romantik: Bildnis einer deutscher Familie*, ed. Elisabeth Rudorff (Leipzig: Staackmann, 1938).

30. *MGG*, s.v. "Philipp Spitta," by Heinrich Spitta.

31. Walter Abendroth, *Hans Pfitzner* (Munich: Langen-Müller, 1935); Werner Diez, *Hans Pfitzners Lieder: Versuch einer Stilbetrachtung*, Forschungsbeiträge zur Musikwissenschaft, vol. XXI (Regensburg: Bosse, 1968); *MGG*, s.v. "Hans Pfitzner," by Wilhelm Moor; Hans-Joachim Moser, *Das deutsche Lied* (Berlin: Atlantis, 1937), pp. 175–85.

32. *MGG*, s.v. "Othmar Schoeck," by Willi Schuh; Werner Vogel, *Othmar Schoeck* (Zürich: Atlantis, 1976); Werner Vogel, *Thematisches Verzeichnis der Werke von Othmar Schoeck* (Zürich: Atlantis, 1956); Werner Vogel, "Othmar Schoeck, ein Schweizer Eichendorff-Komponist," *Aurora* 16 (1956): 59–69.

33. Jürgen Thym, "Die klavierbegleiteten Eichendorff-Lieder von Reinhard Schwarz-Schilling," *Aurora* 38 (1977): 77–86 (with facsimile).

34. *Eichendorff's Sämtliche Werke: Historisch-Kritische Ausgabe*. Founded by W. Kosch and A. Sauer, continued by H. Kunisch (Regensburg: Habbel, 1908—).

35. *Eichendorff-Kommentar*, vol. 1 *Zu den Dichtungen*, ed. A. Hillach and K.-D. Krabiel (Munich: Winkler, 1971).

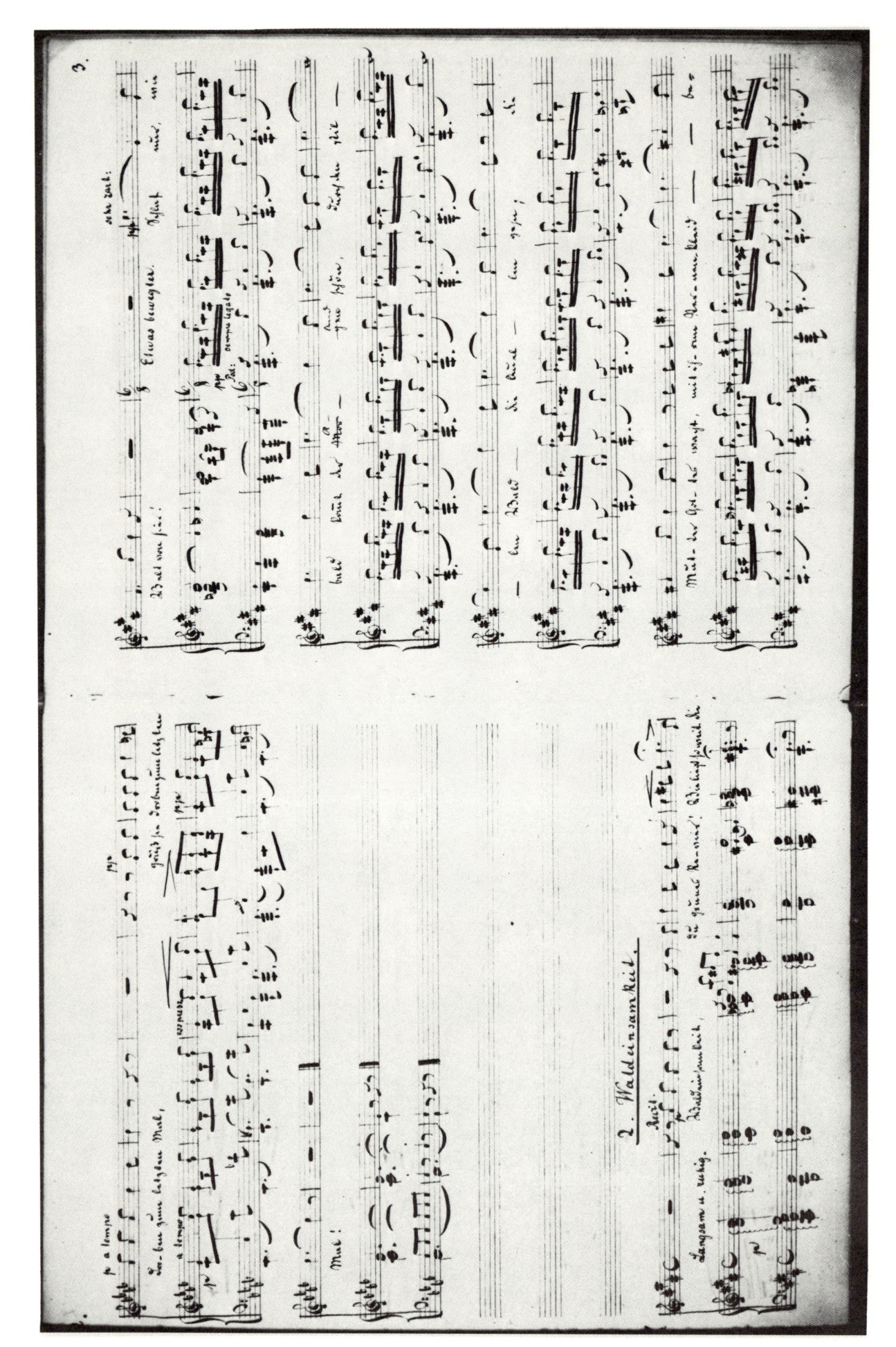

Plate I. Philipp Spitta, *Waldeinsamkeit* [No. 15] Deutsche Staatsbibliothek, Berlin (DDR), Musikabteilung. Mus. ms. autogr., Ph. Spitta 5 (pp. 2–3), 322×250 mm.

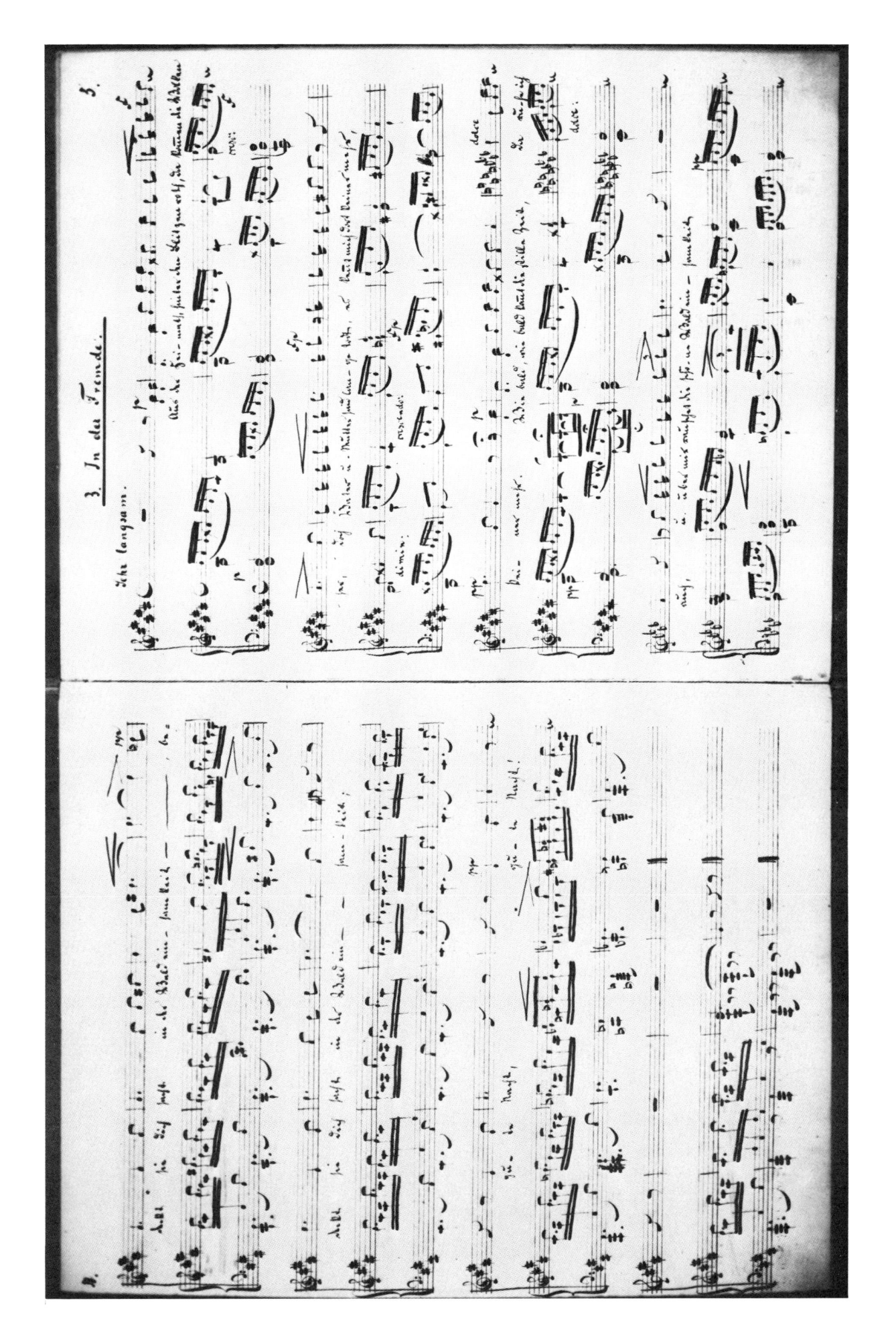

Plate II. Philipp Spitta, *Waldeinsamkeit* [No. 15] Deutsche Staatsbibliothek, Berlin (DDR), Musikabteilung. Mus. ms. autogr., Ph. Spitta 5 (p. 4), 322×250 mm.

Plate II. Philipp Spitta, *Waldeinsamkeit* [No. 15] Deutsche Staatsbibliothek, Berlin (DDR), Musikabteilung. Mus. ms. autogr., Ph. Spitta 5 (p. 4), 322×250 mm.

100 YEARS
OF EICHENDORFF SONGS

[1] Untreue

Friedrich Glück

Andantino

1. In einem kühlen Grunde   Da geht ein Mühlenrad,   Mein Liebchen ist verschwunden,   Das dort gewohnet hat.   Mein Liebchen ist verschwunden,   Das dort gewohnet hat.
2. Sie hat mir Treu versprochen,   Gab mir ein'n Ring dabei,   Sie hat die Treu gebrochen,   Mein Ringlein sprang entzwei.   Sie hat die Treu gebrochen,   Mein Ringlein sprang entzwei.
3. Ich möcht als Spielmann reisen   Weit in die Welt hinaus,   Und singen meine Weisen,   Und gehn von Haus zu Haus.   Und singen meine Weisen,   Und gehn von Haus zu Haus.
4. Ich möcht als Reiter fliegen   Wohl in die blutge Schlacht,   Um stille Feuer liegen   Im Feld bei dunkler Nacht.   Um stille Feuer liegen   Im Feld bei dunkler Nacht.
5. Hör ich das Mühlrad gehen: Ich weiß nicht, was ich will—   Ich möcht am liebsten sterben,   Da wärs auf einmal still!   Ich möcht am liebsten sterben,   Da wärs auf einmal still!

[2] Der Einsiedler

Joseph Dessauer

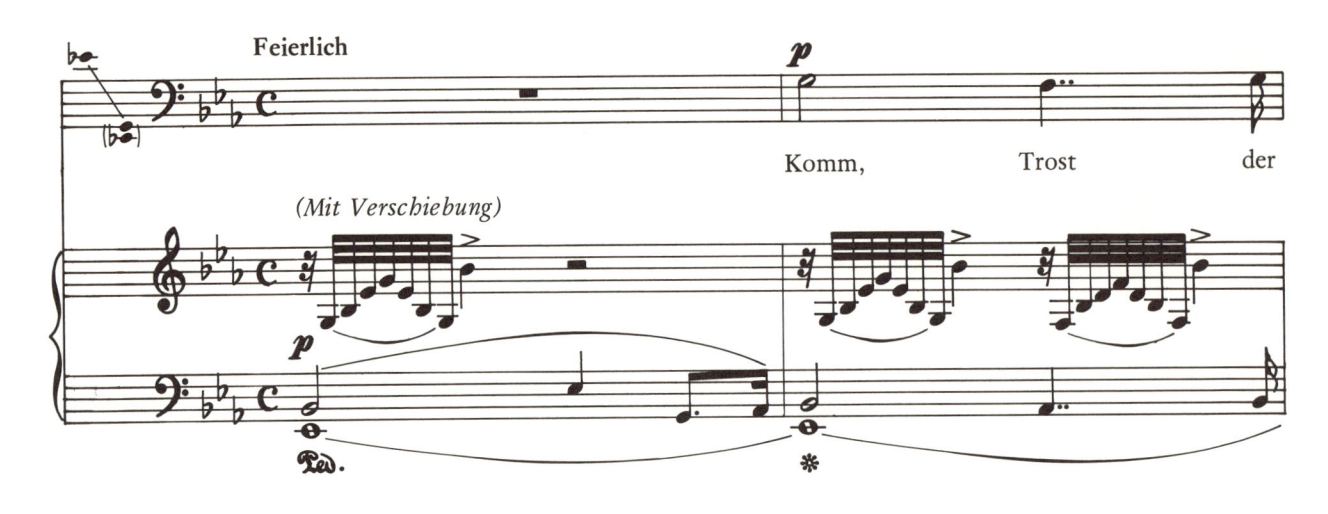

Komm, Trost der Welt, du stille Nacht! Wie steigst du von den Bergen sacht, Die Lüfte alle schla-fen, Ein Schif-fer nur noch wan-der-müd,

Singt ü-bers Meer sein A-bend-lied Zu Got-tes Lob, zu Got-tes Lob im Ha-fen.

(Ohne Verschiebung)

dimin.

Die Jah- re wie die Wol- ken gehn, Und las- sen mich hier ein- sam stehn, Die Welt ___ hat mich ver- ges- sen, die Welt ___ hat mich ver- -ges- sen, Da tratst du wun- der- bar zu mir, Wenn ich beim Wal- des- rau- schen hier Ge- dan- ken- voll ___ ge-

-ses- sen, ge- dan- ken- voll ge- ses- sen, da tratst du wun- der- bar zu mir, wenn ich beim Wal- des- rau- schen hier ge- dan- ken- voll ge- ses- sen, O Trost der Welt! Du stil- le Nacht!

O Trost der Welt! Du

stille Nacht! Der Tag hat mich so müd' gemacht, Das weite Meer schon dunkelt, Laß ausruhn mich von Lust und Not, laß aus- ruhn mich von Lust und Not, Bis einst das

ew'- ge Mor- gen- rot Den stil- len

(Ohne Verschiebung)

Wald _____ durch- fun- kelt, bis einst das

ew'- ge Mor- gen- rot, den stil- len Wald durch- fun-

-kelt, den stil- len Wald durch- fun-

-kelt, den stil- len Wald, den stil- len Wald

rallen.

durch- fun- kelt.

[3] Frühlingsnacht

Friedrich Curschmann
Op. 20, No. 4

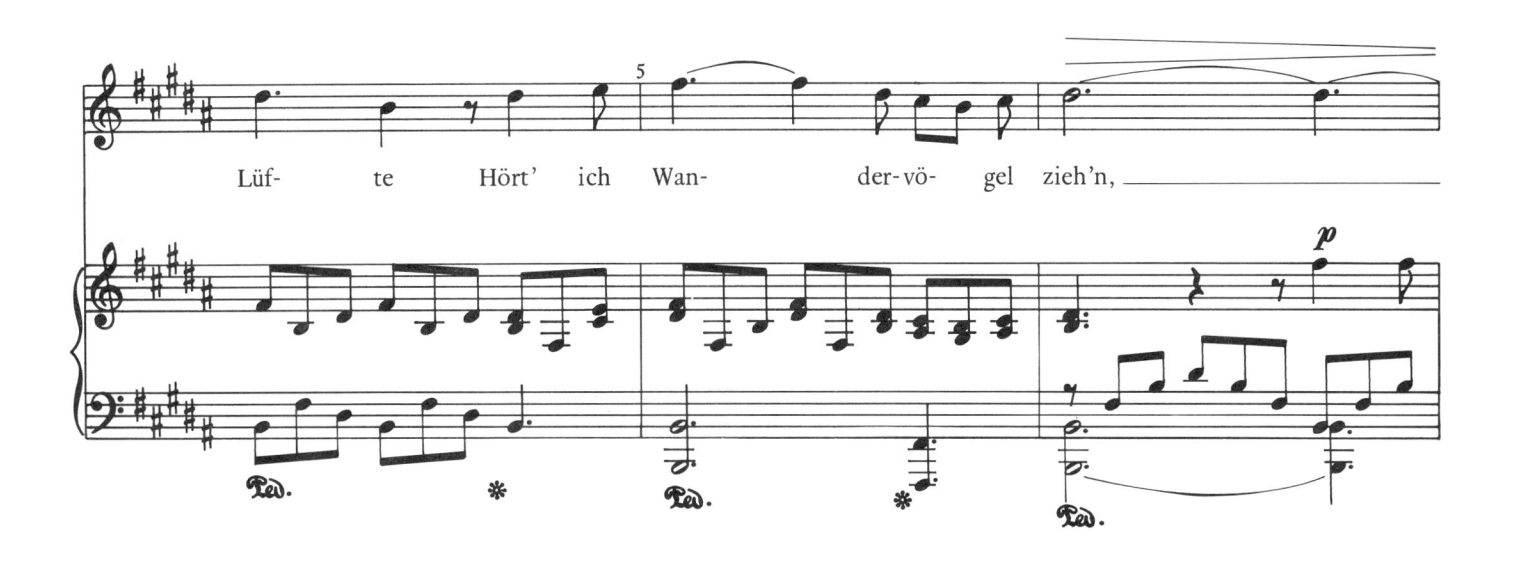

Ü- bern Gar- ten durch die Lüf- te Hört' ich Wan- der- vö- gel zieh'n, Das be- deu- tet Früh- lings-

-düf- te, das be- deu- tet Früh- lings- düf- te, Un- ten fängt's schon an zu blüh'n.

Jauch- zen möcht' ich, möch- te wei- nen, Ist mir's doch, als könnt's nicht sein, als könnt's nicht sein! Al- te

Wun- der wie- der schei- nen Mit dem Mon- des- glanz her--ein. Und der Mond, die Ster- ne sa- gen's, Und in Träu- men rauscht's der Hain, Und die Nach- ti- gal- len schla- gen's: Sie ist deine, sie ist dein, ja, sie ist dein, ja, sie ist dein.

[4] Nachtwanderer

Fanny Hensel
Op. 7, No. 1

Andante con moto

Ich wand- re durch die stil- le Nacht, Da schleicht der Mond so heim- lich sacht

Oft aus der dun- keln Wol- ken-hül- le,

Und hin und her im Tal, Er-wacht die Nach-ti-gall, Dann wie-der al-les grau, al-les grau und stil-le. O wun-der-ba-rer Nacht-ge-sang: Von fern im Land der Strö-me

l'istesso tempo
cresc.
p
25
Gang, Leis Schau- ern in den dun- keln Bäu- men— Irrst die Ge-
pp
Ped.
f
30
-dan- ken mir, Mein wir- res Sin- gen hier Ist wie ein
dim.
p
cresc.
Ru- fen nur aus Träu- men, mein Sin- gen ist ein
35
pp
Ru- fen, ein Ru- fen nur aus Träu- men.
cresc.

[5] Abends

Robert Franz
Op. 16, No. 4

Andantino
Sanft bewegt

A- bend- lich schon rauscht der Wald Aus den tief- sten Grün- den,

Dro- ben wird der Herr nun bald, Bald die Stern' an- zün- den,

Wie so stil- le in den Grün- den A- bend-lich nur rauscht der

Wald. Alles geht zu seiner Ruh,

Tenore ben marcato

Wald und Welt versausen, Schauernd hört der Wandrer zu,

Sehnt sich wohl nach Hause; Hier in Waldes grüner Klause

Herz, geh' endlich du auch zur Ruh.

Tenore ben marcato

[6] Am Strom

Robert Franz
Op. 30, No. 3

Andante con moto
Streng im Tempo

Der Strom glitt ein-sam hin und rausch-te, Wie sonst, noch im-mer, im-mer-fort, Ich stand am Strand ge-lehnt und lausch-te, Ach, was ich lieb-te, war lan-ge fort! Kein Laut, kein

Win- des-hauch, kein Sin- gen Ging durch den wei- ten Mit- tag schwül, Ver- träumt die stil- len Wei- den hin- gen Hin- ab bis in die Wel- len kühl.

Die wa-ren al-le wie Si-re-nen mit feuch-tem, lan-gem, grü-nem Haar,

Ach, von der al-ten Zeit voll Seh-nen Sie san-gen leis' und wun-der-bar.

Sing, Wei-de, sin-ge, grü-ne Wei-de! Wie

Stim- men aus der Lieb- sten Grab,

Zieht mich dein heim- lich Lied voll Lei- de Zum Strom der Weh- mut mit hin- ab.

[7] Der Einsiedler

Karl Reinthaler

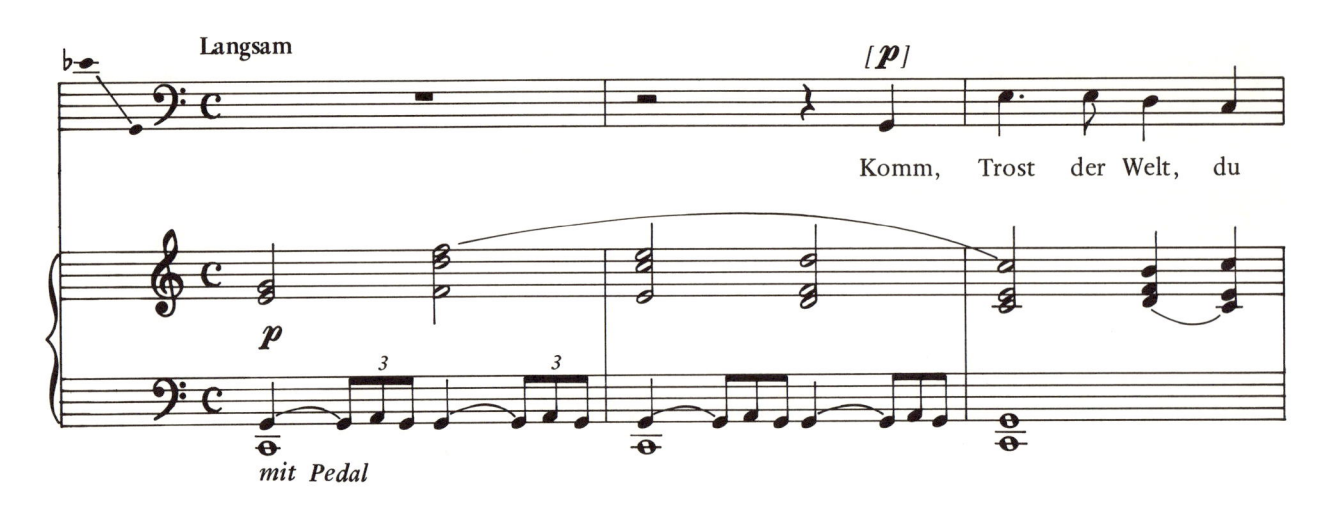

Langsam

Komm, Trost der Welt, du stille Nacht! Wie steigst du von den Bergen sacht, Die Lüfte alle schlafen, Ein

Schif- fer nur noch, wan- der- müd, Singt ü- bers Meer sein A- bend- lied Zu Got- tes Lob im Ha- -fen.

Die Jah- re wie die Wol- ken gehn

Und lassen mich hier einsam stehn,

Die Jahre wie die Wolken gehn

Und lassen mich hier einsam stehn, Die Welt hat mich vergessen,

un poco ritardando

Da tratst du wun- der- bar zu mir, Wenn ich beim Wal- des- -rau- schen hier Ge- dan- ken- voll ge- -ses- sen, Ge- dan- ken- voll ge-

-ses- sen. O Trost der Welt, du stille Nacht! Der Tag hat mich so müd' gemacht, Das weite Meer schon dunkelt, Laß ausruhn mich von Lust und Not, Bis daß das ew'ge

Mor- gen- rot Den stil- len Wald,

den stil- len Wald durch- fun- kelt.

[8] Ich wandre durch die stille Nacht

Theodor Kirchner
Op. 95

O wun- der-ba-rer Nacht-ge- sang: Von fern im Land der Strö- me Gang, Leis Schau-ern in den dun- klen Bäu-men— Wirrst die Ge-dan- ken mir, Mein ir- res Sin- gen hier Ist wie ein Ru- fen nur aus Träu- men, wie ein Ru- fen aus Träu- men.

[9] Die Kleine

Franz von Holstein
Op. 37, No. 1

Ziemlich bewegt, mit Anmut

1. Zwi- schen Ber- gen, lie- be Mut- ter, Weit den Wald ent- lang, Rei- ten da drei jun- ge Jä- ger Auf drei Röß- lein blank, lieb Mut- ter, Auf drei Röß- lein
2. Selt- sam Ban- gen mir im Her- zen Pocht ohn Un- ter- laß, Oft von hei- ßen Sehn- suchts- trä- nen Wird mein Kis- sen naß, lieb Mut- ter, Wird mein Kis- sen

15
blank. Ihr könnt fröh-lich sein, lieb Mut- ter, Wird es drau- ßen still,
naß. Bin ich ei- ne Frau erst ein- mal, Wird es drau- ßen still,
mf
pp
20
Kommt der Va- ter heim vom Wal- de, Küßt euch wie er will, lieb Mut- ter,
Halt den Lieb- sten ich um- schlun-gen, Küß so viel ich will, lieb Mut- ter,
p
sf
dim.
p
poco rit.
1.
25
Küßt euch wie er will.
Küß so viel ich
poco rit.
a tempo
p
sf
rit.
2.
30
will.
a tempo
p
sf
p

[10] Der Morgen

Eduard Lassen
Op. 81, No. 3

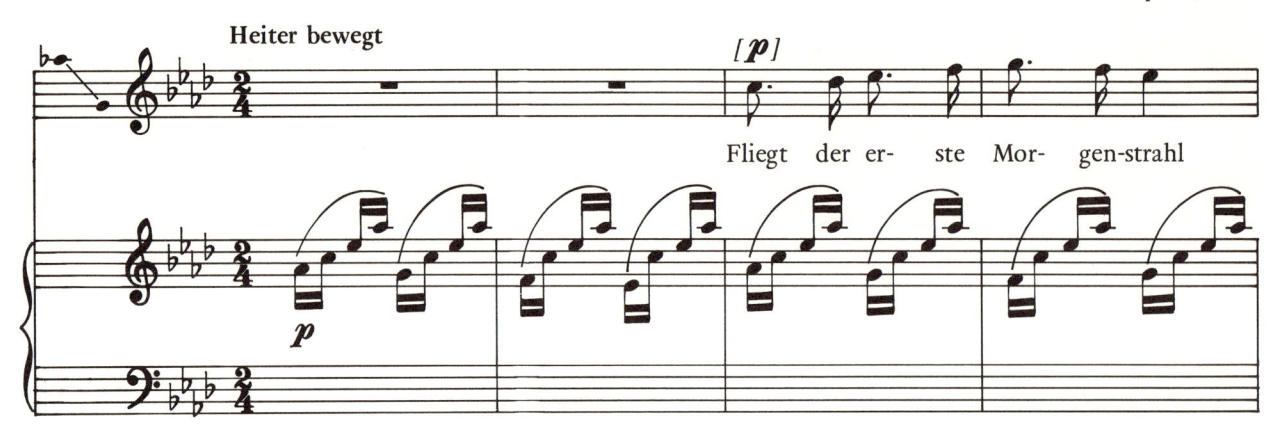

Heiter bewegt

Fliegt der er- ste Mor- gen-strahl
Durch das stil- le Ne- bel- tal, Rauscht er- wa- chend Wald und Hü- gel:
Wer da flie- gen kann nimmt, Flü-

-gel! Und sein Hüt-lein in die Luft Wirft der Mensch vor Lust und ruft: Hat Ge-sang doch auch noch Schwin-gen, Nun so will ich fröh-lich sin-gen! Hin-aus, o Mensch, weit in die Welt! Bangt dir das Herz in kran-kem Mut; Nichts ist so trüb in Nacht ge-stellt, Der Mor-gen leicht macht's wie-der gut.

[11] Waldesgespräch

Adolf Jensen
Op. 5, No. 4

"Der Mitternachtswind heult rauh und düster,
Gleich der Verstorb'nen Grabgeflüster."

Schnell, balladenmässig
Die Charaktere sind genau zu unterscheiden

Rauh und düster

flüsternd, etwas frivol

Es ist schon spät, es wird schon kalt, ___ Was reitst du einsam durch den Wald? Der Wald ist lang, du bist allein, ___

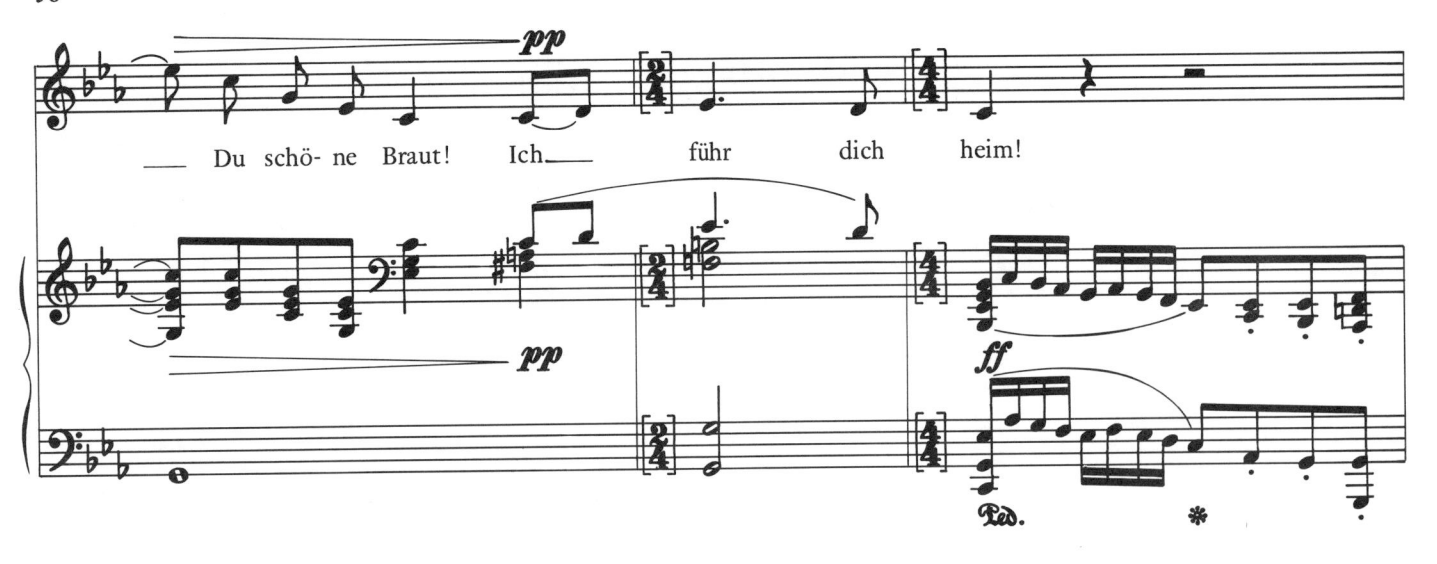

36

Du schö- ne Braut! Ich führ dich heim!

rezitativisch, schmerzlich

"Groß ist der Män- ner Trug und List, Vor Schmerz mein Herz ge- bro- chen ist;

warnend — *p* — *dringend*

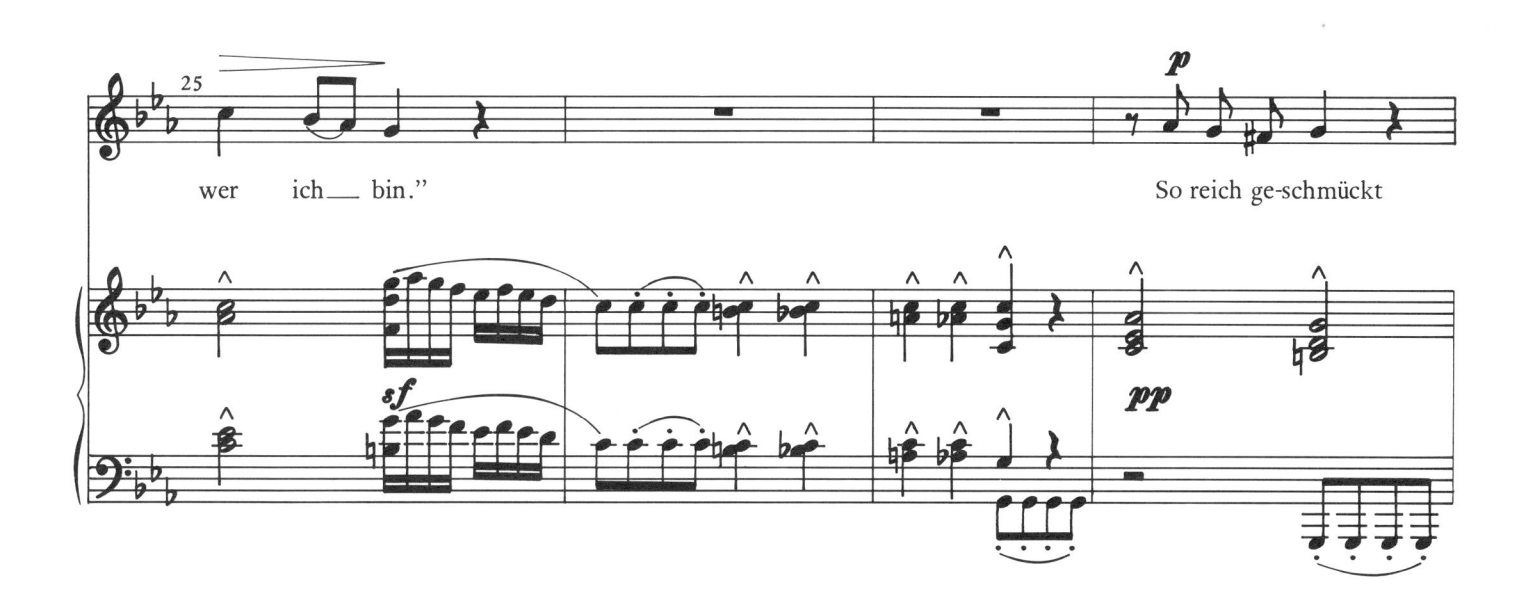

Wohl irrt das Waldhorn her und hin, O flieh! Du weißt nicht, wer ich bin." So reich geschmückt ist Roß und Weib, So wunderschön der junge Leib,

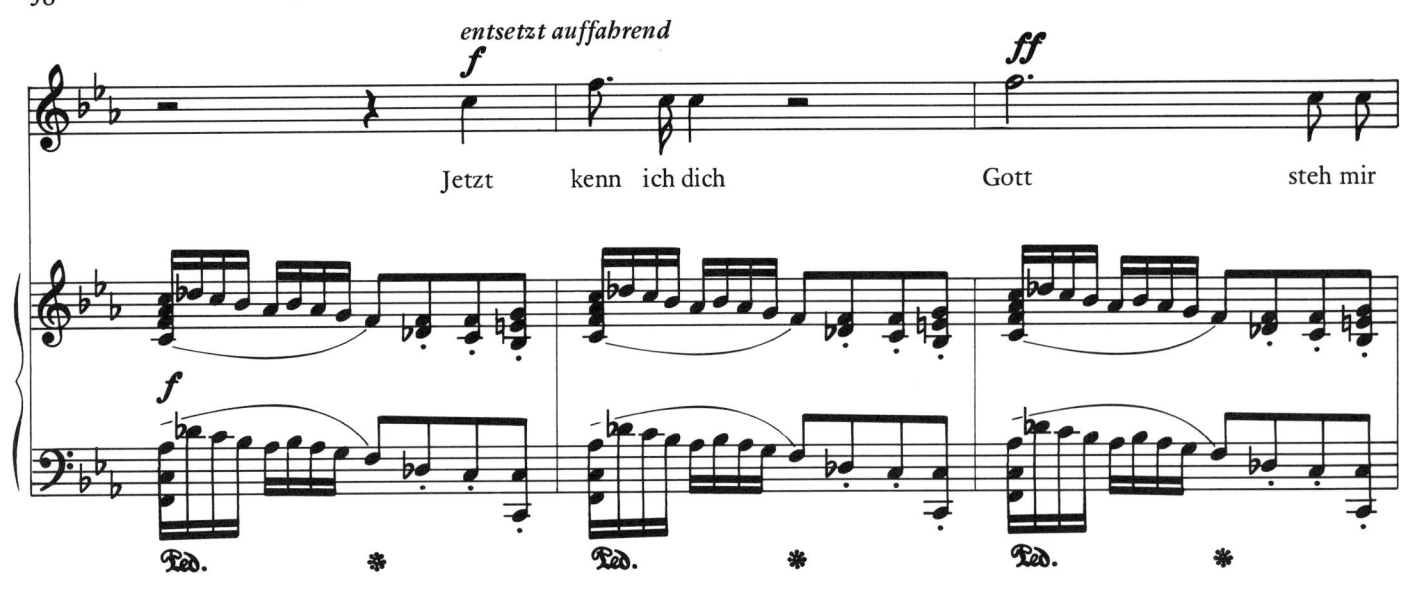

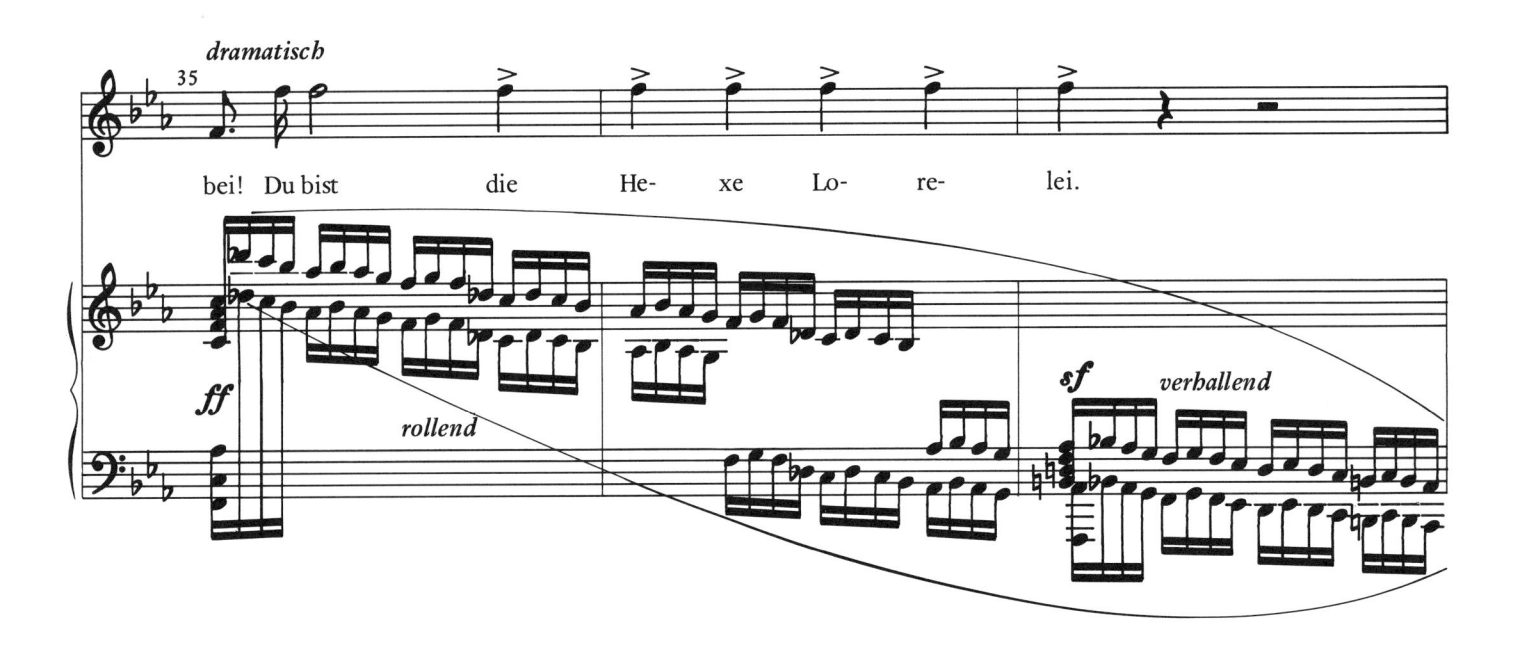

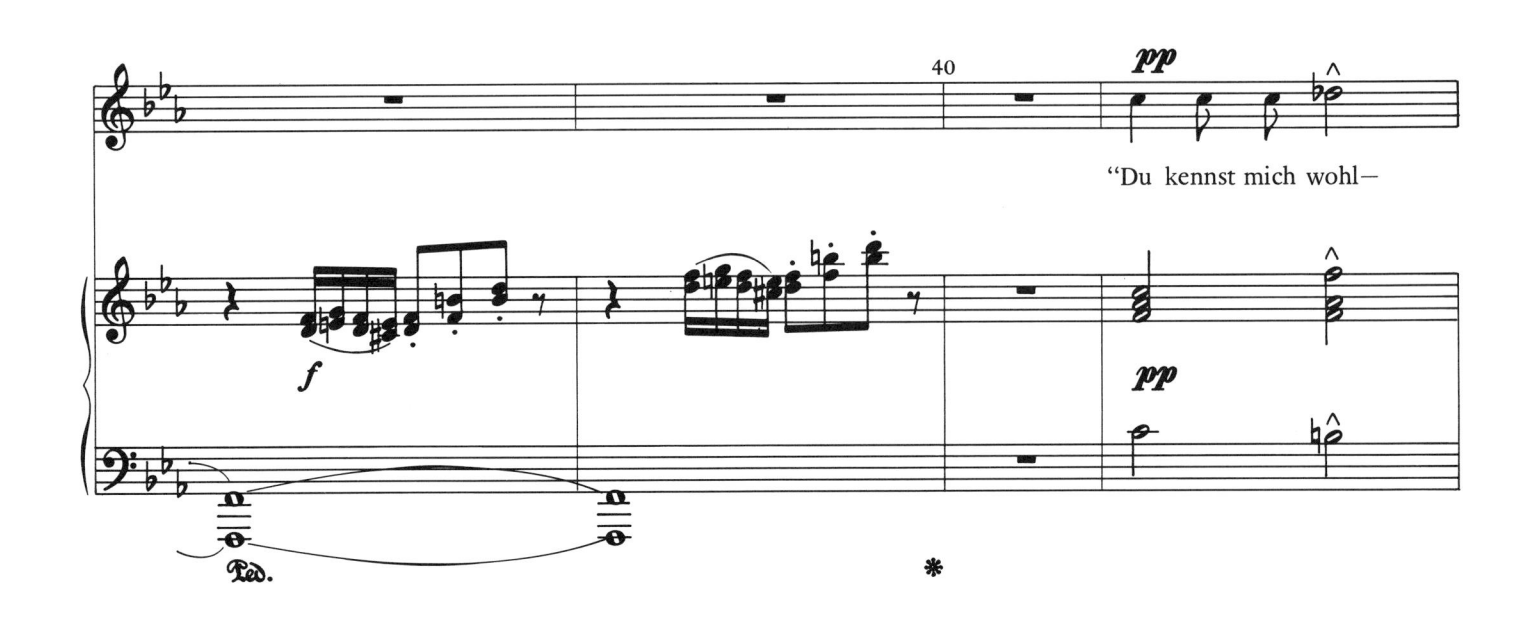

Jetzt kenn ich dich — Gott steh mir bei! Du bist die Hexe Lorelei.

"Du kennst mich wohl—

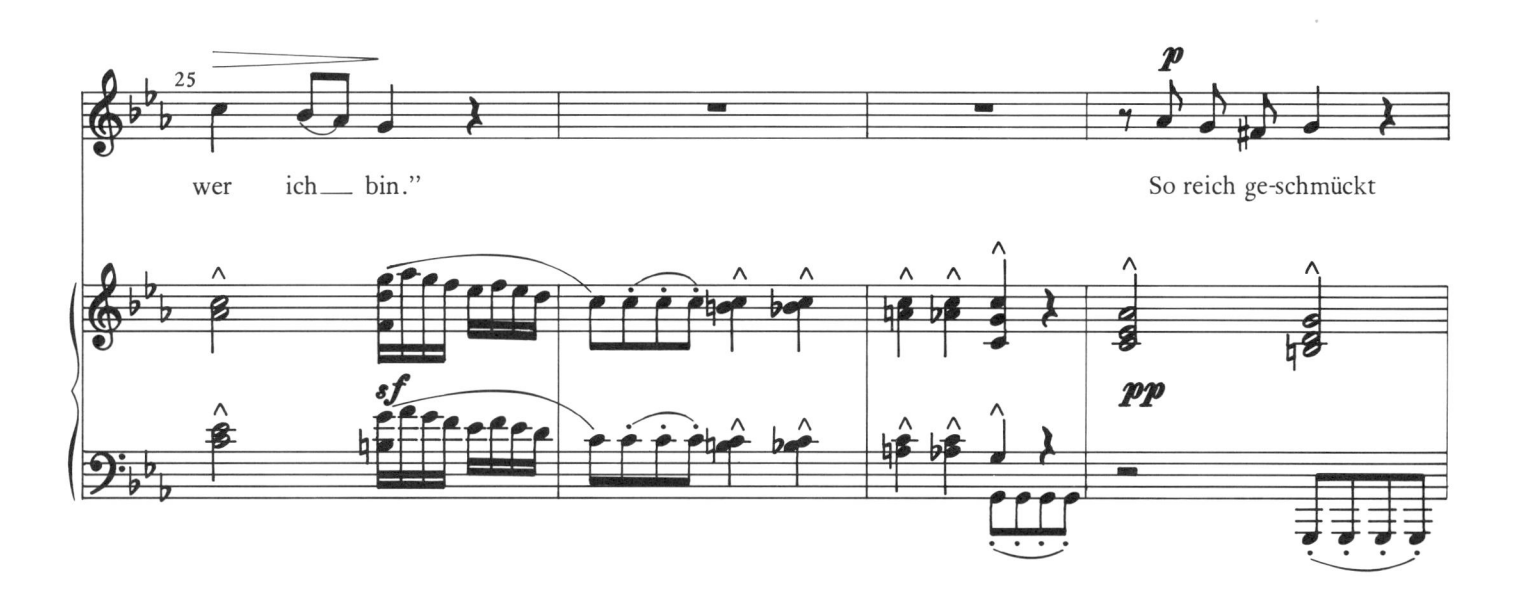

37

warnend   *dringend*

Wohl irrt das Wald- horn her und hin,   O flieh! Du weißt nicht, wer ich bin."   So reich ge-schmückt ist Roß und Weib, So wun-der-schön der jun- ge Leib,

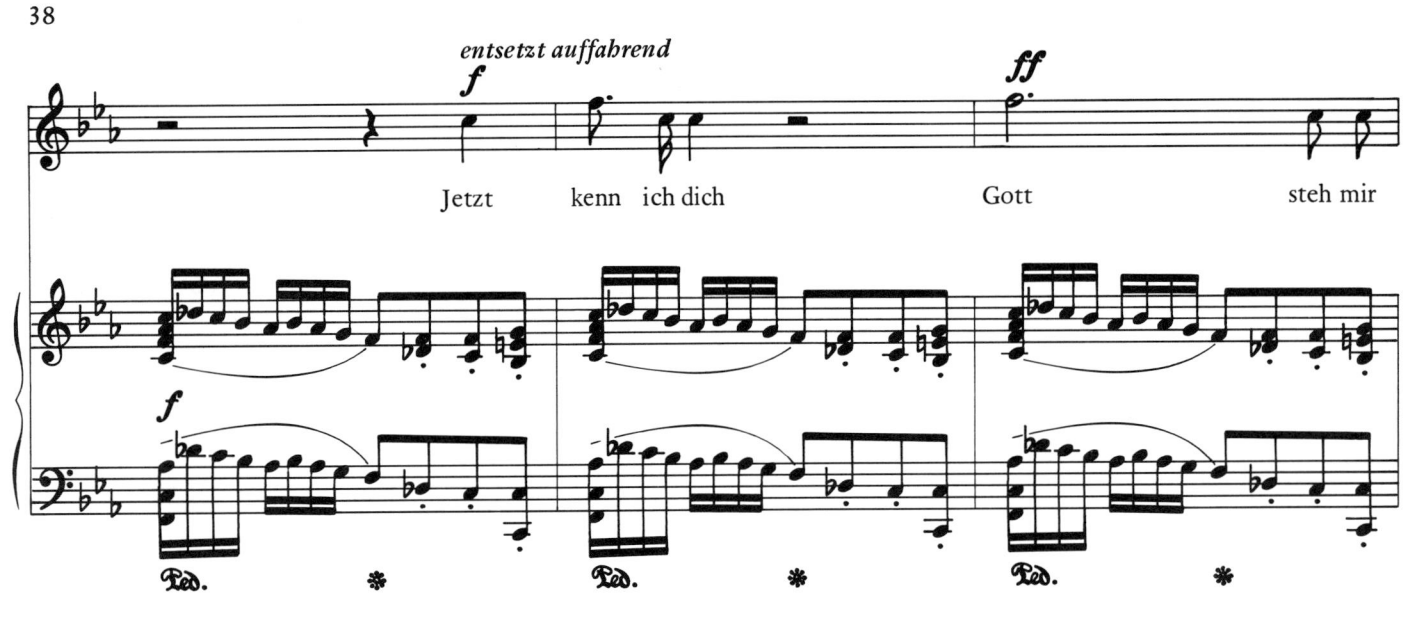

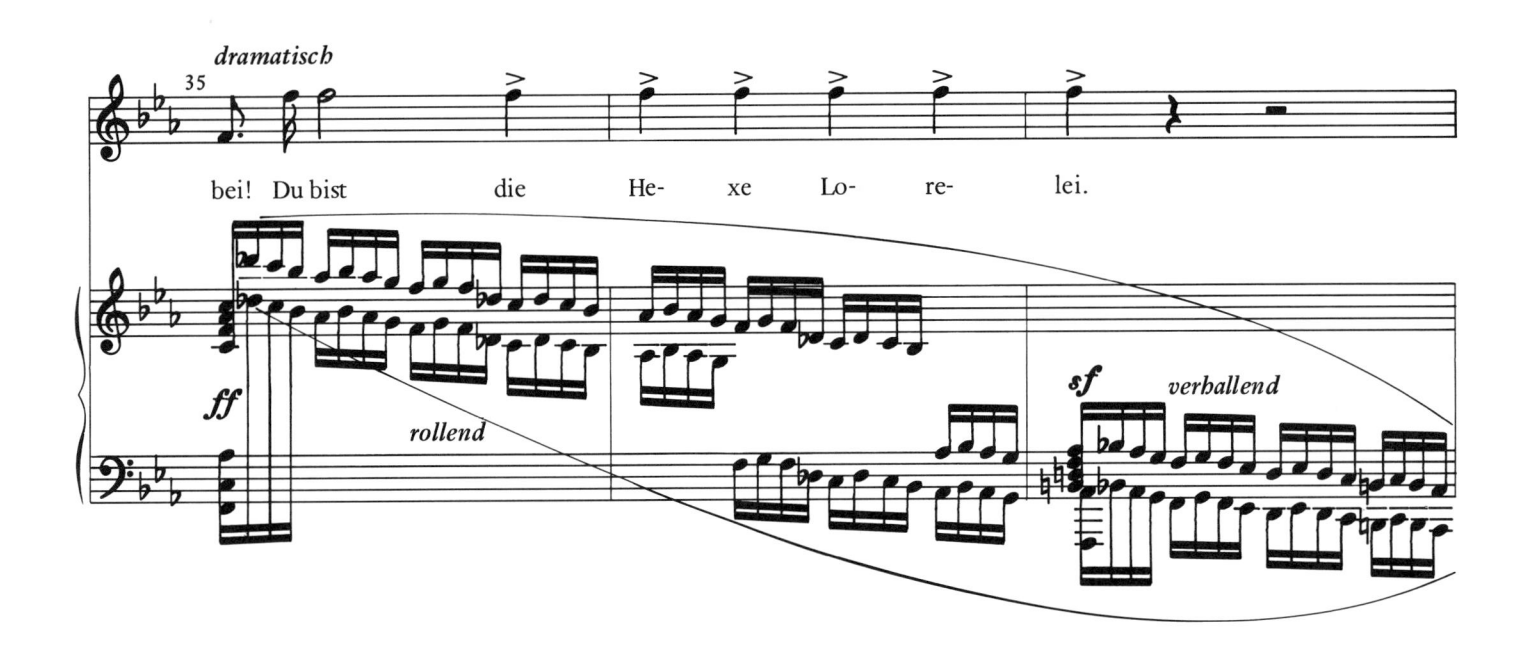

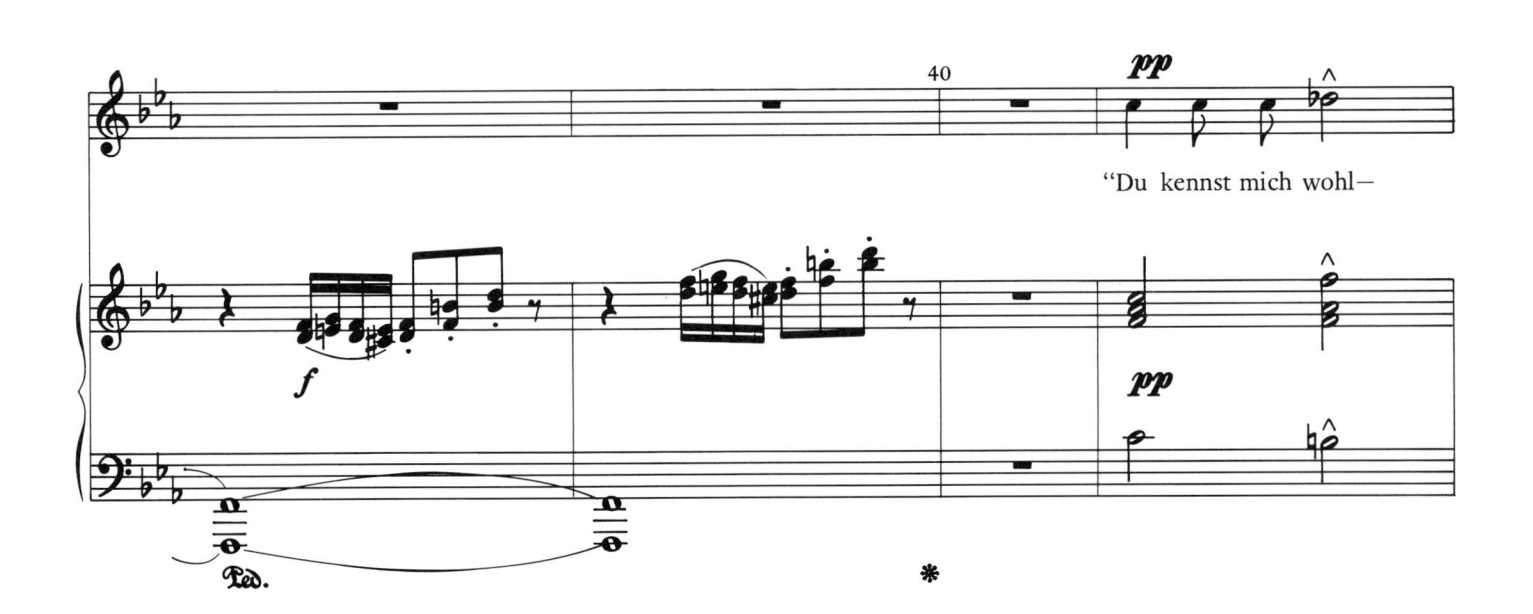

Jetzt kenn ich dich Gott steh mir bei! Du bist die He- xe Lo- re- lei.

"Du kennst mich wohl—

von ho-hem Stein Schaut still mein Schloß tief___ in den Rhein. Es ist schon spät, es wird schon kalt, Kommst nim-mer-mehr aus die-sem Wald!"

[12] Die Nachtblume

Joseph Rheinberger
Op. 22, No. 2

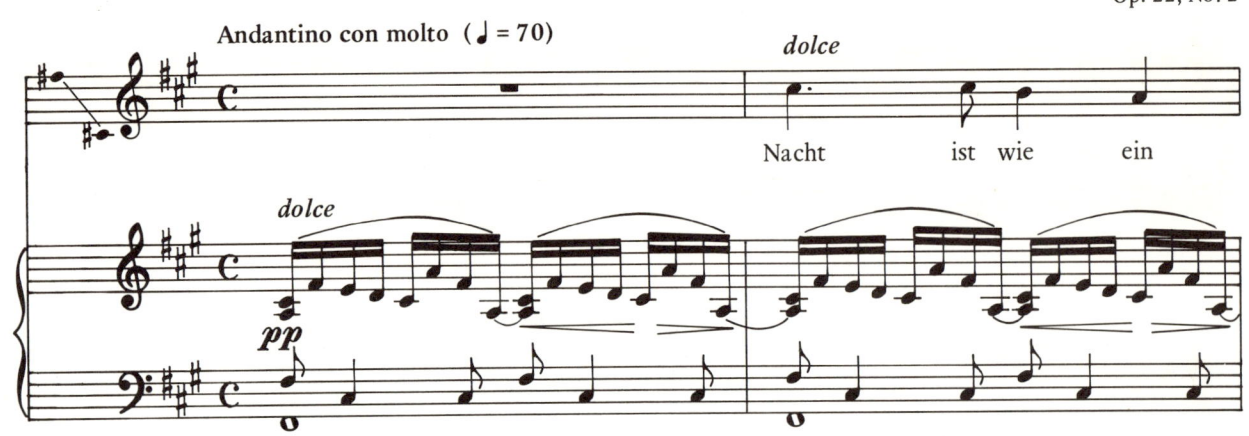

Nacht ist wie ein stilles Meer, Lust und Leid und Liebesklagen Kommen so verworren her In dem linden Wellen-

-schla- gen, in dem lin- den Wel- len- schla- gen.

Wün- sche wie die Wol- ken sind, Schif- fen durch die lee- ren Räu- me, Wer er- kennt _____ im lau- en Wind, Ob's Ge- dan- ken o- der Träu- me? Schließ ich nun auch Herz und Mund, Die so gern den Ster- nen kla- gen: Lei- se doch im

43

Her- zens- grund Bleibt das lin- de Wel- len- schla- gen,

bleibt das lin- de Wel- len- schla- gen.

rit. **Adagio** Nacht ist wie ein

stil- les Meer.

[13] Lockung

Bernhard Hopffer
Op. 22, No. 1

Ziemlich bewegt; frei im Zeitmaß

Hörst du nicht die Bäu- me rau- schen Drau- ßen durch die stil- le Rund? Lockt's dich nicht, hin- ab- zu- lau- schen Von dem Söl- ler in den Grund, Wo die vie- len Bä- che ge- hen Wun- der- bar im Mon- den- schein Und die stil- len Schlös- ser se- hen In den Fluß vom ho- hen Stein?

Kennst du noch die ir- ren Lie- der
Aus der al- ten, schö- nen Zeit? Sie er- wa- chen
al- le wie- der Nachts in Wal- - des- ein- sam-
-keit, Wenn die Bäu- me

träu- mend lau- schen Und der Flie- der duf- tet schwül

Und im Fluß die Ni- xen rau- schen— Komm her-

-ab, hier ist's so kühl.

[14] Frische Fahrt

Ernst Rudorff
Op. 16, No. 2

magisch wilder Fluß, In die schöne Welt hinunter Lockt dich dieses Stromes Gruß.

Und ich mag mich nicht bewahren! Weit von euch treibt mich der Wind, Auf dem

Strome will ich fahren, von dem Glanze selig blind! Tausend Stimmen lockend schlagen, Hoch Aurora flammend weht, Fahre zu! Ich mag nicht fragen, Wo die Fahrt, die Fahrt zu Ende geht!

[15] Waldeinsamkeit

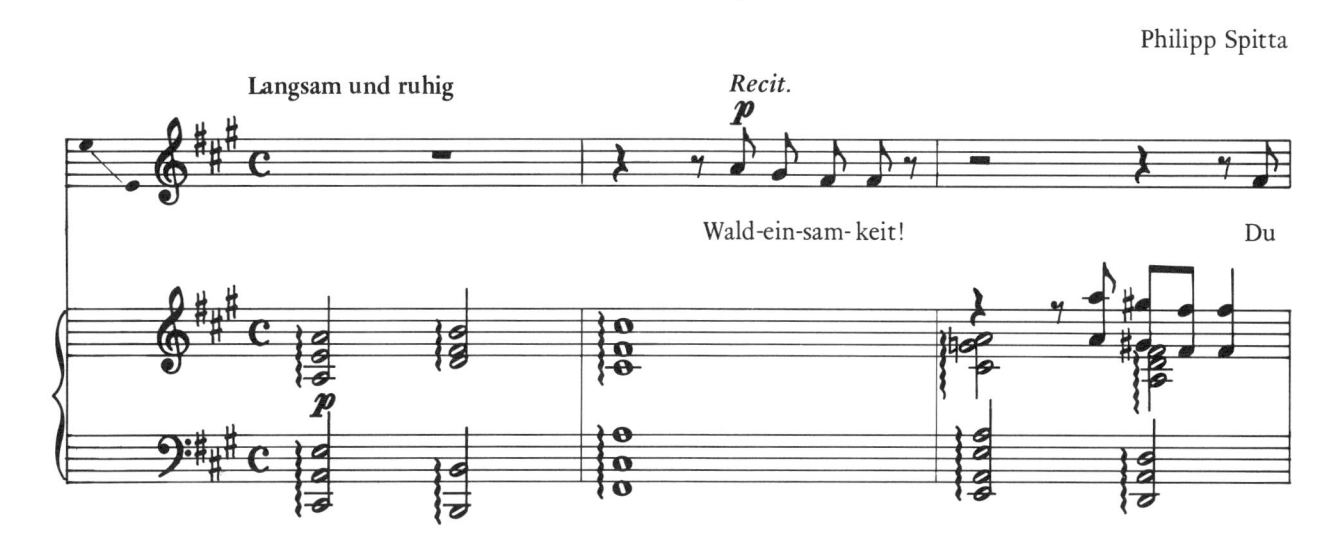

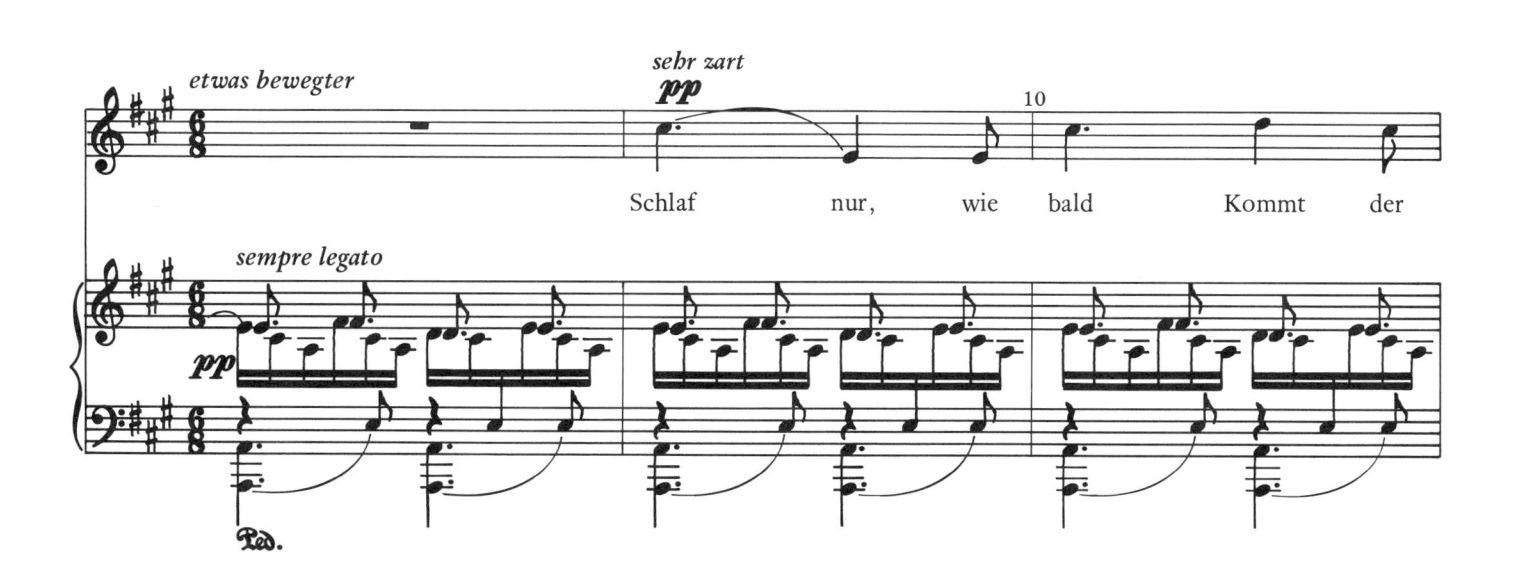

Philipp Spitta

Wald-ein-sam-keit! Du grü-nes Re-vier! Wie liegt so weit Die Welt von hier!

Schlaf nur, wie bald Kommt der

Abend schön, Durch den stillen Wald Die Quellen gehn, Die Mutter Gottes wacht, Mit ihrem Sternenkleid Bedeckt sie dich sacht In der Wald-

-ein- sam- keit, Be- deckt sie dich sacht In der Wald- ein- sam- keit, Gu- te Nacht, gu- te Nacht!

[16] Abschied

Hans Pfitzner
Op. 9, No. 5

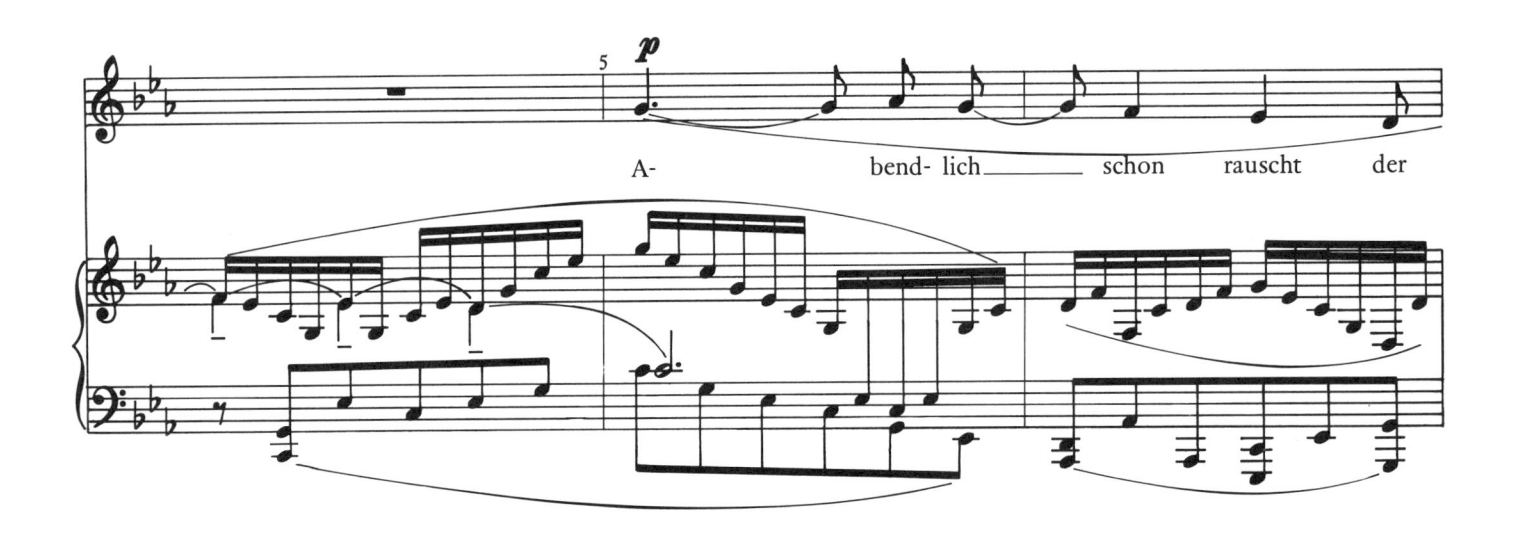

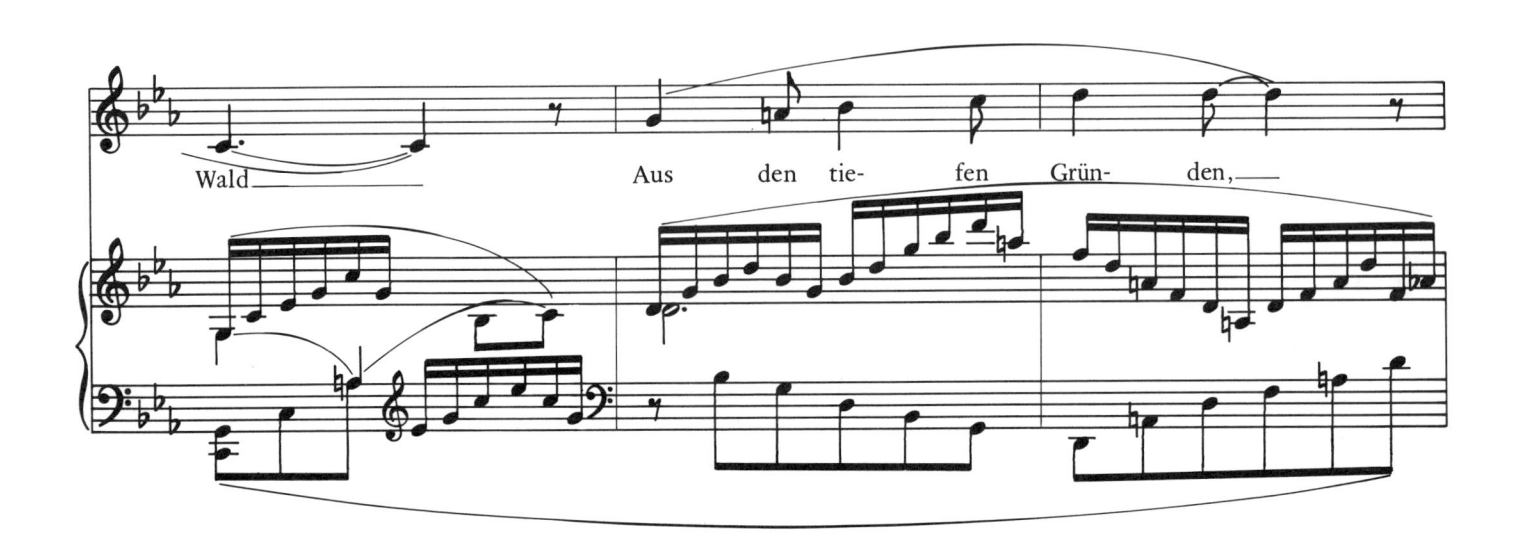

Sehr langsam, leise

*Die Begleitung **ppp** und etwas verschwommen, nur Melodie hervorheben sehr gebunden*

Melodie hervor.

viel Ped.

A- bend- lich schon rauscht der Wald

Aus den tie- fen Grün- den,

Dro- ben wird der Herr nun bald An die Stern- lein zün- den, Wie so stil- le in den Schlün- den, A- bend-lich nur rauscht der Wald. Al- les geht zu sei- ner Ruh,

Wald und Welt ver-sau-sen, Schau-ernd hört der Wan-drer zu, Sehnt sich recht nach Hau-se, Hier in Wal-des grü-ner Klau-se Herz, geh' end-lich auch zur Ruh!

[17] In Danzig

Hans Pfitzner
Op. 22, No. 1

Träu-me-risch der Mond drauf schei-net, Dem die Stadt gar wohl ge--fällt, Als läg zau-ber-haft ver-stei-net Drun-ten ei-ne Mär-chen-welt.

legatissimo

un poco ritardando

Rings- her durch das tie- fe Lau- schen,
Ü- ber al- le Häu- ser weit,— Nur des
Mee- res fer- nes Rau- - schen—
Wun- - der- ba- re Ein- - sam-

-keit! Und der Türmer wie vor Jahren Singet ein uraltes Lied: Wolle Gott den Schiffer wahren, Der bei Nacht vorüberzieht.

[18] Nachtlied

Othmar Schoeck
Op. 20, No. 13

Ruhige Bewegung

p sempre legato

Ver- gan- gen ist der lich- te Tag, Von fer- ne kommt der Glok- ken Schlag; So reist die Zeit die gan- ze Nacht, Nimmt man- chen mit, der's nicht ge- dacht. Wo ist nun hin die bun- te Lust, Des

Freun- des Trost und treu- e Brust, Des Wei- bes sü- ßer Au- gen- schein? Will kei- ner mit mir mun- ter sein? Da's nun so stil- le auf der Welt, Ziehn Wol- ken ein- sam ü- bers Feld, Und Feld und Baum be-

-spre- chen sich,— O Men- schen- kind! was schau- ert dich? Wie weit die fal- sche Welt auch sei, Bleibt mir doch ei- ner nur ge- treu, Der mit mir weint, der mit mir wacht, Wenn ich nur recht an ihn ge-

-dacht. *mit gesteigertem Ausdruck*

mf poco string.   cresc.

Munter und fließend

Frisch auf denn, lie- be

poco rit.   a tempo

f   mf

Nach- ti- gall, Du Was- ser- fall mit hel- lem Schall! Gott

lo- ben wol- len wir ver- eint, Bis daß der lich- te

Mor- gen scheint! Frisch auf denn, lie- be Nach- ti- gall, Du Was- ser- fall mit hel- lem Schall! Gott lo- ben wol- len wir ver- eint, Bis daß der lich- te Mor- gen scheint!

[19] Ergebung

Othmar Schoeck
Op. 30, No. 6

Nicht zu langsam

Es wan-delt was wir schau-en, Tag sinkt ins A-bend-rot, Die Lust hat eig-nes Grau-en, Und al-les hat den Tod. Ins Le-ben schleicht das Lei-den Sich heim-lich wie ein Dieb, Wir al-le müs-sen schei-den Von al-lem, was uns lieb. Was gäb' es doch auf

Er- den, Wer hielt den Jam- mer aus, Wer möcht' ge- bo- ren wer- den,

Hielt'st du nicht dro- ben Haus! Du bist's, der, was wir bau- en,

Mild ü- ber uns zer- bricht, Daß wir den Him- mel schau- en—

Dar- um, so klag' ich nicht.

[20] Marienlied

Reinhard Schwarz-Schilling

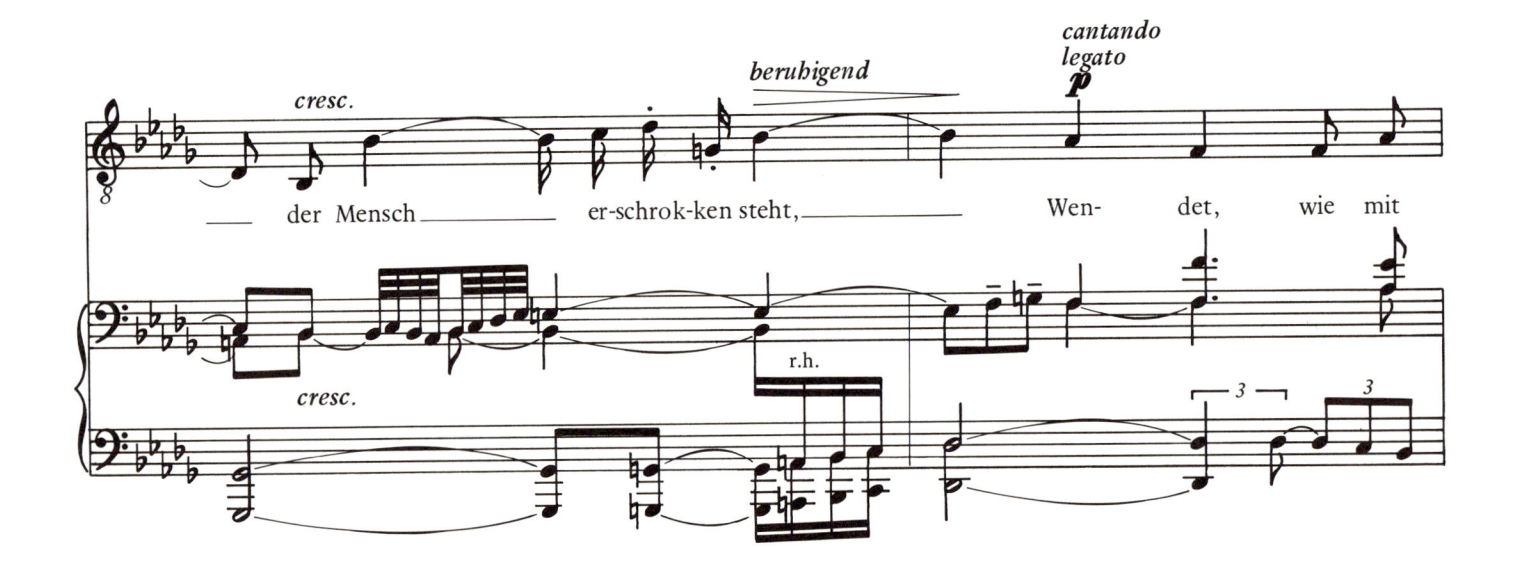

Ruhig, jedoch nie schleppend
(zu Beginn ♩ = ca. 50)

Wenn ins Land die Wet-ter hän-gen Und der Mensch er-schrok-ken steht, Wen-det, wie mit

(♩ = ca. 54)

Glok-ken-klän-gen, die Ge-wit-ter Dein Ge-bet,

Und wo aus den grau-en Wo-gen Wei-nend auf-taucht das Ge-fild, *etwas zurückhaltend* **Sehr ruhig** (♩ = ca. 48) Seg-nest Du's vom Re-gen-bo-gen-Mut-ter, ach, *ziemlich stark verbreiternd* **Tempo tenuto** (♩ = ca. 40) wie bist Du mild! *kaum zögernd* **zurück ins Tempo I** (♩ = ca. 50) Wenn's einst dun-kelt auf den Gip-feln und der küh-le A-bend sacht nie-der-rauscht in den Wip-feln: O__ Ma-ri-a, heil-ge Nacht! Laß mich nim-mer wie die an-dern, Dek-ke zu der letz-ten Ruh Müt-ter-lich den mü-den Wan-drer Mit dem Ster-nen-man-tel zu.

M2.R23834 v.5 Q
100 YEARS OF EICHENDORFF
SONGS.

M2.R23834 v.5 Q
100 YEARS OF EICHENDORFF
SONGS.